WAYS
OF
PRAYING

John C. Edwards SJ

FAMILY PUBLICATIONS

WAYS OF PRAYING
by John C. Edwards, SJ

First published	1982
Revised and reprinted	1988
Reprinted	1996

ISBN 1 871217 01 6

published by
FAMILY PUBLICATIONS
77 Banbury Road, Oxford OX2 6LF
Telephone: 01865 514408

cover design by
Benedictine Sisters at Turvey Abbey

printed in England by
BPC Wheatons Ltd, Exeter

by the same author:

Ways of Forgiveness
Ways of Loving
A New and Special Way

Fr John Edwards was born in Sussex and was educated at Ampleforth and the Royal Naval College, Dartmouth. He went to sea in 1947 and served in the Korean war, leaving the Navy in 1953 to seek his vocation with the Society of Jesus. He was ordained Priest in 1964 and continued his studies in Rome. Since 1968 he served in parishes and more recently in retreat work and parish missions which have taken him to the USA, Iceland, New Zealand, Mauritius and various countries in Africa.

Contents

Introduction

Elijah, you will remember, one day was down and out – he wanted to die. Then an angel brought him food. In the strength of it he was able to walk for forty days and forty nights.

In September, 1974, a number of priests and I made a retreat under the direction of Fr John Edwards, S.J. In the strength of it, ever since, we have been stepping out briskly on the paths of the Lord.

In this booklet Father sets out some of the guidelines we found so helpful. His basic theme is simple – in all the circumstances of the day see to your prayer life and it's 'All systems go' in your spiritual life. 'It works' he assured us. Many of us will bear witness to the fact.

A work of caution. A great friend of mine, St Anthony of Padua, once preached a marvellous sermon which radically renewed the lives of hundreds of people – or was it thousands? Read that sermon to-day and you may well wonder how on earth it could have touched and inspired so much so many.

The sad truth is that words, even those of Holy Scripture, may make little or no impact on us unless we are properly disposed – unless we are genuinely interested, attentive, eagerly receptive and prepared to act on the graces offered as we read or listen.

All this to suggest that before starting to read the pages of this booklet, or any other spiritual book, it is a 'must' to pause for a moment and pray that the Holy Spirit in his goodness will speak to us and inspire us as we read. Try it. As Father says: 'It works'. Or rather the Holy Spirit works within us. The results can be astonishing!

I pray you will enjoy and profit as much from reading these pages as we did listening to Fr John Edwards, S.J.

Stephen McGill,
Bishop of Paisley.

Preface

Much of this booklet has been printed before, in the *Personal Renewal Series* and by the Catholic Truth Society. I am grateful to the latter for allowing it to be reprinted by Family Publications.

Even more I thank Cardinal Hume for his kind words of encouragement which appear on the back cover, and the late Bishop McGill for his Foreword.

It is hoped that *Ways of Praying* may serve as a 'follow up' for people to whom I have given missions and for religious whom I have directed in retreats. Companion booklets are *Ways of Loving* (about marriage, sex, celibacy, consecrated chastity), *Ways of Forgiveness* (on confession) and *A New and Special Way* (for apostolic religious). Later there may be *Ways of Knowing* (understanding the Faith).

Most of us need encouragement in prayer. This book tries to give it, saying only: "If God is real, we must pray. We're not asked to enjoy it, only to do it. And *this* is why . . . and *these* are possible ways . . . "

John C. Edwards, S J

One:

Ways of God's Presence specify styles of Prayer

Prayer is loving attention to God. To attend to God with love we must advert to his Presence. It therefore helps clarity to list some of the ways God can be said to be 'present', or occasions of special 'access' to him. To each of the presences there is, more or less and with much overlapping, a style of prayer appropriate. It may seem pedantic and contrived to list these 'presences' and to suggest corresponding prayer-styles, but if we mean to pray it does help to know what we set out to do.

1. God is present *in all things*, as he is their Creator. To attend to God in creation, that is at all times, can be called *Informal Prayer.*

2. Christ *in his redeeming moment* brings a special presence. He 'ever lives to make intercession for us.' This intercession is the continual action before his Father's face of all his earthly life – pre-eminently his Passion, Death, Resurrection. This is still operative because Christ as man is what he is now because of the rewarding perfection by the Father for his actions on earth. Our joining to this moment is the *Mass*. Here is a 'method' of prayer which in very fact 'makes' God present in a unique way.

3. God is present, because active, in his *Word*. The true use of Scripture is a way of prayer.

4. Christ says he is present 'where two or three are gathered together in my name.' The special access to God available in a group can be called *Group Prayer.*

Christ is present in his Body, the Church. Wherever the Church is and acts there is an approach to God, a union with him. Now the Church acts, and indeed 'happens', pre-eminently at the Mass, itself the prime example of Group Prayer; but closely involved with Christ's Body are the next five presences.

5. Christ is present in the *Blessed Sacrament*, a presence and an

operation obviously linked vitally to the Mass, for the Blessed Sacrament is what it is, moment by moment, because of the Mass at which it was consecrated. The prayer style appropriate can be called *Devotion to the Blessed Sacrament*, an implicit thanksgiving or preparation for Mass.

6. Christ is present and works in all the *Sacraments*, and does so through his Body the Church, with special directness and certainty. Each of the *Sacraments* is, or ought to be, a special style of prayer.

7. The Church prays officially as Christ's Body, deputed to praise the Father in his name; this brings a special presence of Christ, which is not vitiated even by the sinfulness of his members. This prayer is the *Office*, or *Prayer of the Church*. It still remains a prayer of the whole Body even when an individual officially deputed, priest or enclosed religious, says it alone.

8. Christ through the Church uses material things as a source of contact or presence when an object is 'touched' by him in a special way. There is a wide spectrum of prayer here which can be summed up as *Prayer by Sacramentals;* it includes use of Ikons, relics, holy water and much else. In a broad sense even unblessed objects can be used as quasi-sacramentals.

9. Sometimes God can be known to be present at the meeting of men who join together as witnesses of actions or words which they intend to bind them and to commit them definitively. God too is witness, but he can be trusted to do more than observe – he can say 'as you intend it, *I make it so.*' This is the *Liturgy*. It covers not only the Mass, Sacraments, Benediction, the Office but in principle many lesser actions including what can be called 'para-Liturgies'.

(An explanation: the dividing line between 'Liturgy' and 'Para-Liturgy' is a fine one. Mass is a Liturgy; strictly speaking – according to some Roman Documents – Benediction is a Liturgy. Is a Corpus Christi procession . . . ? Hardly: it is a para-Liturgy. The detail of children strewing flowers before the Blessed Sacrament is definitely para-liturgical. Kissing the Cross on Good Friday is a liturgical act; during a Penance Service, it is para-liturgical.)

Now all contact with God is through Christ and therefore, provocative though it may seem to say so, through the Church. But the following two 'presences' can be considered apart from the action of the Church.

10. God is *present in each man*, who is either alive with Christ's life, or if not present to the Father because in Christ, at least open

to the redemptive love of Christ's Passion. The prayer-style here can be called *Private, formal prayer*. When we 'say our prayers', the object really is – though we may not think of this – that beyond or through or even in spite of the method used, we should be setting up the conditions in which God could make his presence known to us, if he wished.

11. God is present in a special way when we receive *guidance from the Spirit*. There is in fact a specific style of prayer devised to enable us, given certain presuppositions, to discern the Spirit's movements. It is the Ignatian *Examen* in five points.

It is possible therefore to distinguish in a rough and ready way eleven styles of prayer appropriate, more or less, to different 'presences' of God. They admit a great deal of subdivision if one feels inclined – a certain amount is listed in Appendix 1 – but obviously even the main prayer-styles are not mutually exclusive. The Mass, for example, contains nearly all 'presences'.

Once one has grasped that presence and prayer go together, foolish talk that restricts attention to God to only one 'presence' ('Liturgical prayer is the only thing that matters'; 'I do all my prayer while listening to music'; 'I can pray only when walking in the park'; 'If one does a good day's work, one has done all the prayer one needs') becomes less possible. 'Prayer' is a word like 'movement'; it covers many different activities. There is a time for walking, swimming, going in an aeroplane or turning somersaults; we must use the movement appropriate to the circumstances. So with prayer, we must pray as appropriate to the presence of God.

Appendix 1 lists the styles, and 'methods' of prayer suitable to them. Subsequent chapters explain some of them.

Two:

Formal Private Prayer: Theory

1. The place of formal private prayer

This rather formidable description covers what we do alone when we 'say our prayers' or 'make our meditation'. It can be defined in various ways: 'raising the mind and heart to God', 'loving awareness of God'. The mechanics of it is basically this: either we are alive with Christ's life, present in him before the Father, or we have deprived ourselves of this relationship through serious unrepented sin; if we are in grace we are potentially open to experience Christ's presence, if he wishes to make it known to us; if we are not in a state of grace, we have a special call on the saving love he exercised on Calvary and are the object of his special attention. In either case, there is a special 'presence' of God available to us.

We must attend to this presence regularly and at some length. It is madness, let alone bad manners, to be so close to Christ – identified with Christ even – in the depths of our being and in every cell of our body – without adverting to it. A man, to be human, must respond to beauty: here is the source of all beauty and it is within us. To be deaf, blind, incapable of enjoying music or painting or the presence of a loved one, is a dehumanising misfortune. To be unable or unwilling to pray is far worse.

The purpose of life is to do God's will, to serve him. For enclosed religious the primary service of God is prayer. It is the purpose of their life, and all else is a means to this end. For other people the service of God is various and prayer is only one of the means of serving him. But in either case prayer is indispensable. A Carmelite will eat, sleep, work, recreate in order to be able to pray: someone 'in the world' will pray, eat, sleep, work in order to be able to do the particular service that God requires. The real difference is that in enclosed orders all the circumstances are designed to help contemplative prayer, whereas other people have the same invitation to contemplative prayer without the same aids, which are sacrificed to allow a more varied service. In both cases the aim is the service of God; but in the case of the enclosed the service has been focussed into one single end. It is hard to tell, but among religious it seems the gifts of prayer are in fact evenly spread among enclosed and unenclosed.

With regard to prayer, time is important. All religious should be scrupulously faithful to the quantity specified by their Chapters or Congregations. I suggest that lay people should think in terms of at least fifteen minutes daily. Without a serious, often painful, amount of time given, it is difficult to see how certain graces of prayer are going to be open to us.

A 'defence' of private prayer is elaborated in chapter 5.

2. Pre-requisites for prayer

Obviously awareness of the presence of God 'within' is all important. For this, the presence of grace, the life of Christ, is clearly going to alter the style and feel of the prayer. It may be that the first necessity for being able to endure private prayer is a good confession. Of course the man in sin, as has been said above, can and must pray, but the necessary desire to meet God would normally include the urge to repent.

Perhaps the immediate pre-requisite for prayer is in fact prayer itself. Religious who prepare their prayer the night before could feel easy in their conscience if they devoted that time to praying. Important too is peace of body and mind. But more vital than anything is the quality of the life we lead outside our prayer. It is just not possible to want to meet God inside prayer when one has been avoiding his known will outside. The condition for prayer, and the only measure of 'success' in prayer, is the level of unselfishness in ordinary life.

To sum up the pre-requisites for prayer:

(1) Desire to meet God: includes repentance; love of others.

(2) Intent to pray.

(3) Peace.

3. *The practical importance of prayer*

Something about this has been said above. If it is remembered that prayer is not primarily asking, nor a matter of thoughts, nor a matter of words, but a question of *loving attention to God*, the obligation becomes clearer. There are however two very practical points to be considered.

First, unless we pray we are hardly likely to worship God in other ways – for instance, to go to Mass. The motive for Mass-going is, in the last resort, love of God. It is not likely to be the eloquence of the sermon or the zestful liturgy which will draw us. Not for long, not without a deeper motive. Nor will parental pressure forever urge the young. Either they want to be present at the Last Supper, Calvary, and in union with the risen Christ, or they don't. If they do, it presupposes love; love presupposes contact; contact with God, meeting God, needs prayer.

More fundamental still is the fact that to have the Faith logically and theologically presupposes prayer. The act of Faith is frightening: 'O my God, I believe in you and all your Church doth teach, *because you have said it* and your word is true'. The motive of credibility is not knowledge of theology but experience of God's word: in other words, prayer. If my Faith weakens, the only remedy is that I should pray. You cannot believe someone you have not met.

From this it follows that prayer is not an optional extra for good people who have time to kill, but the prime necessity for all – very much including sinners. Serious prayer is the first thing to be taught, not the last, in the religious lesson.

4. *The place of will and intellect*

Prayer is loving attention to God. The attention exists for the love. Loving is done by the will; it is a question of wanting. Love is not feeling, nor is it thinking. If prayer were a matter of thinking it would follow that the man with the better brain would, other things being equal, be better at prayer. Also it would mean that the best way to pray would be to get down to a desk and draft an essay for God to see. This is nonsense. I do not have to think holy thoughts for God, or run a film-show in my mind to entertain him. My thoughts about God are in fact no holier than my thoughts about football. It is not the content of my thoughts that make my prayer. The place of imagination and intellect in prayer can be as small as is necessary to allow my wanting, my will, to keep me engaged.

5. Meditation and Contemplation

For John of the Cross, meditation is to move the thought from one point to another, to allow the will to operate. For Ignatius it is the same, but he practically confines the term to periods of prayer devoted to sin: he expects a man to 'meditate' perhaps fourteen times during the first of the four weeks of the Exercises. The Exercises might have 150 periods of prayer; meditation accounts for perhaps 14 of them.

Ignatius uses the word contemplation, which he expects will involve some discursive movement, but in a more formless way probably than John of the Cross' 'meditation'. Ignatius uses the word almost always to describe browsing, restful gazing, being steeped in, involved in attention to a mystery of our Lord's life. It might or might not be classified as meditation by John: probably not, since Ignatius insists on one 'staying where one finds what one wants'.

Both men would expect meditation to give way to something non-discursive, non-reasoned. John insists that meditation is possible only for beginners. I myself have never found anyone who could meditate in any structured way more than a few times without some distress. Structured, coherent, discursive thinking during prayer must be a very rare thing indeed.

The reason is psychologically quite simple. The mind cannot rest happily on thoughts which are familiar unless they happen to be favourite ones: it rebels.

Contemplation, in John's language, can be synonymous with the Dark Night. Night, because the thinking is blind. Blind, because it flinches away from the painful, over-familiar, thought pattern. An excellent book on all this is *The Prayer of Faith*, by L. Boase, S.J.

Contemplation can be either arid or consoled. If it is arid, then the methods described below can be used. If it is consoled, Ignatius' rule of 'staying where one finds what one wants' applies: in other words, one adopts elementary good manners to God, which incidentally involves doing what seems most attractive – even though it means apparently doing nothing.

9

Contemplation can be infused or acquired. Acquired contemplation is where one exerts oneself to hang on to God. It is usually arid. Infused contemplation is where God is operating more or less directly. It may be consoled, to a small degree or strongly. If it is arid, then the behaviour in it is exactly as described above. One would hardly know in aridity whether it was 'infused' or not. Nor in fact does it matter in the least.

This outline is obviously *simpliste* and condensed. But I believe it is adequate for self-guidance in prayer. It boils down to this:

If prayer is sweet and consoled – go on doing whatever you are doing. If it is hard and dry, hang on to God with your will. To do this, you will probably find useful some of the methods listed and described in other chapters.

6. *Trinitarian and Christocentric Prayer*

There are two basic types of awareness in prayer. The first is that we should somehow sense that we are addressing, acted on, attending to, Christ. This is the way most of us are taught to pray as children. It is the slant of St Bernard, St Francis, St Bonaventure. It is called 'Christocentric' because centred on Christ.

The other type of awareness has a different attitude to Christ. It is not that we feel we attend to him, rather that we are in him and held thus before the Father. It is really a more logical form of prayer, since it follows the approach of the Mass. Few of the Mass prayers are addressed to our Lord, the whole action is towards the Father; Christ however is not neglected – how could he be? He *is* the Sacrifice; he is doing the praying.

With this latter, 'Trinitarian', prayer there may be a sense that the Spirit, Christ's spirit, carries our prayer to the Father.

Neither of these attitudes can be thought of as better than the other: the only reason for mentioning them is that it can help to identify one's basic slant in prayer, which may shift to and fro at intervals. To identify whether one is at the moment Christocentric or Trinitarian can help one to avoid going against the pattern God is inviting one to follow, with consequent pain and aridity. One's 'use' of the Blessed Sacrament for example, or a mystery of Christ's life, or the Passion, could be altered to suit whichever slant is predominant.

A sudden, pronounced, noticeable and enduring shift from one style to another is sometimes the mark of the first touch, or a renewed touch, of infused prayer.

It is interesting that devotion to the Sacred Heart at its most traditional is open to both Christocentric and Trinitarian prayer. 'See this Heart,' says our Lord 'wounded for men's sins: make reparation.' This is Christocentric. But the saints and mystics of the Sacred Heart always experience and see what the theologians only know; the fact of grace. Christ exchanges hearts with the beholder, or puts a spark of Its Fire into them. And then, of course, being animated with *his* life, afire with *his* love, dwelt in by *his* heart, their gaze and their love becomes directed where his is — to the Father. And this is Trinitarian.

Three:

Formal Private Prayer: Preliminaries

1. *Attitudes in prayer and the primacy of praise*

To 'hold an attitude' in prayer is for most a more profitable exercise than 'thinking'. For many people the task is simply to adopt some fairly simple mental stance, some spiritual gesture, some attitude of soul: to slip a colour-filter into the stream of will-light that we mean to direct to God.

Here are some basic 'attitudes' in prayer, of which there will be amplification later.

(1) Adoration;

(2) Contrition or Reparation;

(3) Thanksgiving;

(4) Supplication or Intercession or Petition;

These could be adapted to a 'purgative', 'illuminative' or 'unitive' approach as explained in 5. below. Later on, when methods are treated, it will be seen that one word held in the heart may be sufficient to provide a prayer-attitude before God.

Here, all that needs to be said is that Praise is too often neglected as an attitude. Praise is an aspect of Adoration, for Adoration is best described as saying to God 'You are wonderful'. It is, therefore, essentially a lover's response. It is to admire the splendour of the loved one: 'This person, independently of any benefit I may receive, even if I were not to exist, demands as of right the tribute of admiration; this I now have the privilege of proclaiming, face to face, in the very gaze of the one I love.' This, before God, is adoration. It is the whole-time activity of heaven; in Christ, and with his power, we will be doing it for all eternity. We ought to be doing it now.

It is a response to Glory. This is commonly described as 'full advertence to God, with praise'. Obviously Christ is the full Glory of the Father; but we are in Christ, and he owes praise through us. In fact for practical purposes Adoration may be a less useful word than Praise. Adoration sounds static; Praise is active.

The phenomenon of Pentecostalism and the 'charismatic movement' can teach us something. Pentecostals see the need to praise, indeed it is to be able to praise God without constriction that they welcome the 'gift of tongues'. The great advantage of praise is that it is unselfconscious. One does not need to be anxious about one's performance, the point about praise is that one wants to do it, welcomes the chance. One is totally engaged with the other person.

The picture of praise is this: three young Spanish peasants who gather under the first-floor window of a noble, beautiful, wealthy, unapproachable girl. There is a grille, and the shutters are closed. It doesn't matter. She may even be out of town: she certainly will not call out to them or even look at them. It does not matter. They cannot sing well; the guitar is missing a string. It does not matter. The point is, *they are able to praise her*, and that is all that matters. So should we be before God. Notice this: *they sing with a smile on their faces*. Praise belongs to joy.

This means in practice that if I want to pray, I am praying. And that means that if I am 'putting in the time' I am almost certainly praying. Love, wanting, is a measurable activity – and the measurement is not of intensity of feeling, prolixity of words, intelligence of thoughts, but fixity, intention, of will. A mother sitting up with a sick child is lovingly aware, even though she may be thinking of something else: what is she doing at 2 a.m. by the bedside, if she is not loving?

The only contact we have with God is in Faith. The only feeling to which a man is entitled in prayer – not that God cannot ravish him if He wishes – is the conviction, certainty, of God's presence. A conviction need not involve any emotion: it can be cold and featureless. Faith can feel precisely that. Prayer can be a matter of doing nothing – but doing it with God. It is the will, the wanting, the hanging on to God with the will, that matters. Whatever thoughts or feelings may be washing through me do not matter; providing I do not divert my will, as I would if I took up a novel and started reading it, no distraction could possibly destroy my prayer.

2. *Basis: God loves us. Certainty in Faith*

(i) *God loves us*. He is neither incompetent nor malicious, for he is all-powerful and he is my tender-loving Father. Therefore he is to be praised and thanked for everything. For *everything*. If I feel he cannot be praised and thanked it is because deep down, whatever I say with my lips, *I secretly* think he is incompetent or malicious. Now when one begins to pray one really must be sure one is praying to the One True God and not to Baal or Moloch ... Part of the discipline and routine of the 'act of the Presence of God' and of preliminary recollection is to find in one's heart a 'smile in response' to God. The smile may be through tears ... but it must be there.

(ii) *Certainty in Faith*. Faith gives knowledge. Faith is certain. Faith is not primarily a feeling. Faith is certain because of God's authority. If God ever revealed there must be, somewhere, at some level, at least in some conditions, certainty. No certainty, no revelation. A Christian who is in no respect certain can hardly be a Christian. A Catholic who cannot bring himself to make the Act of Faith (O my God I believe in you and all your Church *teaches*, because you have said it and your word is true), or at least to want to make the Act of Faith, is, well – not a Catholic.

If I seek to make contact with God in prayer without, if I am a Roman Catholic, trusting the Roman Catholic Church as His Body and the interpreter and custodian of his revelation, without trusting its Magisterium, without therefore finding certainty in revelation, without therefore trusting that he has in fact revealed, without therefore trusting him – the situation becomes ridiculous.

Aridity in prayer, mere 'going through the motions', neglect of prayer, can often be attributed to not knowing that God loves me, or not really concretely believing he is trustworthy. In other words to failure in Faith, Hope and Charity. 'Techniques' of prayer are useless unless there is the substance.

3. *The limited usefulness of methods: the importance of freedom*

Prayer is a question of hanging on to God with the will. Unless he himself is pleased to hold us engaged, the problem remains of how to do it. Bluntly, often, how to fill in the time. For this, methods can be useful.

There is one 'method' that is all-important, it is to do what seems most sensible. Wherever one 'finds God', St Ignatius would say, there one must stop. Wherever one last 'found God', there is the best place to start. It is obvious really. If God is engaging the soul in some way, it is rank bad manners to try to interest him in something else: 'Excuse me, Lord: I realise you may want me to rest still in the knowledge of your presence, but I intend to run through a bit of Teilhard in order to keep you interested'. It does not matter how often, how long, one goes to one attitude or one line of a psalm, one thought, one state of awareness, provided it is a 'finding of God'.

If however it is not a question of being held by God – of gentle joy and peace, even if this is weak and thin – then it is a matter of us providing some framework, structure, vehicle, carrier, method, which enables the will to hang on. This is where methods come in. The ones listed in Appendix 1 para. 10. and described in chapter 5 are honest and possible. Their purpose is quite simple: to set up conditions whereby God could, if he wished, make his presence known to us.

4. *The two levels of attention*

When a man is at a cocktail party he is having to try to be amusing, and he is having to act as if he is entertained by the conversation of others. It can be hard work. He is at the 'first level' of attention. When he is at home he can rest in silence with his wife, in complete awareness of her. He is at the 'second level' of attention.

A man copying out music concentrates on it; he attends to it at the 'first level', the 'thinking level'. Listening to Beethoven he attends to the music certainly, but in an entirely different way. He is at the 'second level'.

In prayer we normally want to be at the second level.

Physical helps to it: a straight back (mainly for better breathing); absolute stillness; as many muscles as possible quite loose. Above all: eyebrows *not* furrowed; lips *not* pursed; jaw *not* clenched.

15

Without this physical tension a line of thought cannot be sustained. And at prayer we want to be *below the thinking level*, at the 'second level' of attention.

5. *What to pray about*

Unless it is a question of intercessory prayer, the best rule has already been given: 'start the prayer where you last found God'. However if something more explicit is needed, two suggestions are offered.

The four ends of the Mass are basically Adoration, Contrition or Reparation, Thanksgiving and Supplication (or Intercession or Petition). These are suggested as 'attitudes' to have in prayer, and are detailed in the chapter on Structures.

Then too a possibility is to take one of four petitions appropriate to the classical phases of the spiritual life, and to start the prayer with them. This is the pattern of prayer in the four weeks of the Spiritual Exercises of St Ignatius: the exercitant, except for a few special periods of prayer, is praying for an hour at a time four or five times in the day and night for basically one of four graces:

'Purgative': 'Lord, that I may hear you tell me to repent and be converted, and that I may have a horror of sin and wrong choice.'

'Illuminative': 'Lord, that I may stand face to face with you, and understand what your right choices are, and do the same.'

'Unitive': (*a*) 'Lord, that I may be broken, shattered, with sorrow at what happened to you, and be one with you in the cross.'

(*b*) 'Lord, that I may be totally, permanently afire with unselfish joy at your great joy in the Resurrection.'
'Lord, that I may be with you before the Father, and that your Spirit may pray through me.'

6. *Aids to attention*

The task in prayer, if task it is, is to hold the will, the love, on to God. For this it can help to enlist as much of God's creation as we can to help us, or at least to disarm God's creation from pulling us away. Here are some means to this, some hints, only to be used if they in fact prove useful. We are talking still about formal private prayer.

(i) *External*
    (*a*) Silence.
    (*b*) 'Numinous environment' (if I am not in Church, I can at least have a crucifix in sight).

(ii) *Body*
    (*a*) Position (described later).
    (*b*) Hearing (let the sounds drop away).
    (*c*) Sight (close the eyes, or use a relaxed and steady gaze).
    (*d*) 'Second level of attention' (cf. no. 4 above).

(iii) *Internal*
    (*a*) The will: advert to God's presence.
    (*b*) The intellect: advert to a mystery of our Lord's life.
    (*c*) The imagination: *gently* absorb the 'colour' or flavour of the scene, letting it steep into one.
    (*d*) The affectivity: knowing that the 'mystery' is in very truth present, because the risen Christ is present, take the 'attitude' appropriate.

All this cannot help looking like a cock-pit check list prior to take off. It may prove unnecessary. But it might help. Those who know the Spiritual Exercises will note that (*a*), (*b*), (*c*), (*d*) of the last paragraph correspond to the Preparatory Prayer, the History, the Composition of Place, the Grace to be asked for, which Ignatius recommends.

7. *The three uses of vocal prayer*

(i) To attend to the meaning of the words.
This includes very short ejaculatory prayer, or more lengthy spontaneous talking to God (not as easy or as common as one might think – at least, for more than a couple of minutes at a time) or the recitation of set prayers, or the reading of prayers from a book. (Quoist, Hollings, Gullick are authors much used.) For praying this way with set prayers, long, slow-paced, solitary walks are ideal.

17

(ii) To ponder words or phrases.
Here the words, say, 'Thy Kingdom come', are dwelt on, repeated, and their content gazed at. This is as near the traditional kind of 'meditation' as most of us get. St Ignatius' 'Second Method of Prayer' is of this sort.

(iii) To use the words as a vehicle for something else.
Here the words are not being thought about. They are repeated continuously (as, usually, with the Hail Mary in the Rosary) or rhythmically (as in the Breathing Method or Jesus Prayer). They do their work without being thought about: they pacify one level of consciousness, and their content somehow seeps through into a higher level, preparing the will to rest easily in God. The use of words in this way is common in the major non-Christian religions as well, and one which it is well to take very seriously.

8. *The use of the body in prayer*

Most major religions use psychosomatic techniques in prayer. Christians, because they realise that God cannot be contacted through skills or art but only by his gift, may not realise that they too use the body. Robes, vestments, organ music, singing, plainchant, stained glass, incense, singing Hallelujah, laying on of hands – in one denomination or another among Christians all these things happen – all impinge on the senses. It is right to try to set up the external conditions in which one might become aware of God. But the body itself needs to be set up.

Basic to every position of body in formal prayer must be external reverence, because if the body conveys a note of irreverence, the spirit will not so readily be open to God's touch: soul and body are one. Here are commonly used positions:

(i) Kneeling. Back upright, elbows not used as support.

(ii) Standing. Upright, back straight; absolutely still; head gently bowed; finger-tips at nostril or mouth level, and touching them – the hands joined in the 'Dürer's praying hands' position.

(iii) Squatting. Shoes off; open the heels; sit back on them; A cushion if necessary under the instep. Hands loose in the lap.

From time to time the body can shift on to one or other foot, the cushion replaced as necessary.

(iv) Walking. For formal prayer, as opposed to informal, it is best to walk slowly, and best to guard the eyes. It will not normally permit the 'higher' states of prayer, but it will prevent sleep. (Not that sleep at prayer necessarily stops the will operating, or must necessarily be avoided at all costs . . .) Walking fast, or with eyes unguarded, will obviously permit 'informal' prayer, but hardly formal.

(v) Sitting. Always still; best to have the back upright.
In all the positions the relaxation of face muscles is important; eye-brows, lips, jaw.

(vi) Lying Down. Face down or face up. Always still. Note: it is one thing, a good thing, to pray while one is in bed: it is another thing, not good, to go to bed in order to pray!

Four:

Structures in Prayer, and Methods

1. *Structures*

(i) *Aids to Attention.*

This 'structure' has been outlined in chapter 3 no. 6.

(ii) *A.C.T.S./A.L.T.A.R.*

These mnemonics can help by pinning the mind down, or by setting an attitude of soul. The method is to make ACTS of:

A Adoration (or Praise).
C Contrition (or Reparation).
T Thanksgiving.
S Supplication (or Asking, Petition, Intercession).

Or, using the other formula, to make ACTS of:

A Adoration (or Praise).
L Love.
T Thanksgiving.
A Asking.
R Reparation.

The ALTAR formula reminds one that all prayer is connected with Christ's sacrifice. But the ACTS one is more intriguing:

(*a*) It is linked with the four ends of the Mass.

(*b*) Using the image of Christ on the cross, from the foot I can look upwards to Christ, or through Christ's heart let my prayer be carried by his to the Father. This is *Adoration*, to say 'You are wonderful'. Then I lower my eyes down his Body, down the wood where his Blood has flowed, to myself. My prayer turns to *Contrition:* 'You are wonderful, and it is for me you suffered; I am sorry.' Then my gaze follows his right arm, where he points to the past. With sin forgiven, my prayer can turn only to *Thanksgiving:* 'You are wonderful, and have done wonderful things for me.' His left arm points to the future. My prayer becomes *Supplication:* 'You are wonderful; and because you are, I confidently ask you for all my needs.'

(*c*) In eternity there is the eternal 'white light' prayer, Adoration, Christ's praise of the Father. But one may think of time, and fallen creation, breaking that white light into a spectrum: the three 'colours' of Contrition (present moment), Thanksgiving (past) and Supplication (future) become visible.

2. Methods – vocal

Chapter 3 no. 7 outlines styles of vocal prayer in the widest sense. Here two obvious methods are listed, primarily to reassure people who use them.

(i) *Talking to God*

What is really meant is 'Chatting to God'. Many people can do this quite easily. It is a fine method, but it is not normally possible for more than a few minutes or where the subject matter did not impinge directly on me. I can chat to God about work, worries, people – but not directly about Himself very easily. My day, yes; his day, when he fed the five thousand – rarely. Consequently the subject matter and the time devoted to the approach of God, although eminently worthwhile, are circumscribed.

(ii) *Listed intercession*

Quite a large proportion of believers find a valid prayer-style here. They have long, fixed lists of people and things to pray for, and work through them. If this form of prayer helps and is easy – proved by one's being able to do it without undue difficulty – it is excellent. But it should not be the only style of prayer, nor should one feel compelled to keep it up forever.

3. *Methods – primarily for Bible prayer*

Apart from prayerful reading, styles of 'derivative prayer' are listed below. Here only the last two methods are detailed.

   (i) *Meditation.* (cf. chapter 2 no. 5).

   (ii) *Pondering the words of vocal prayer.* (cf. chapter 3 no. 7).

   (iii) *Rosary* (cf. *My Rosary,* Harty, O.P., Rosary Crusade: *Five for Sorrow, Ten for Joy,* Ward).

   (iv) *Stations of the Cross.*

   (v) *Application of the Senses*
> (Note that Sight, Hearing, Touch are used imaginatively, the sense of Smell and of Taste 'spiritually'. That is to say, the imagination applies itself to see, hear, all that the Mystery of our Lord's life shows it, and so with the sense of touch; while the senses of taste and smell are applied by holding up the scene to the Father. The man at prayer opens himself to the 'scent' and 'flavour' of the holocaust of Christ's love which the Mystery shows, a more passive way of attending to God.)
>
> Much is written about the application of the senses and the method or even mysticism involved. I have only met one person who ever actually prays that way by choice.

   (vi) *Ignatian Contemplation*
> When faced with Ignatius' injunctions to 'gaze at the persons, see what they are doing, ponder what they say,' most people try to make a sort of film-show in their mind. Dissatisfaction at once arises: it is hard work; it is boring to keep doing it (and each film-show is over in a few seconds): one feels frustrated because one doesn't know if the scene was *really* like that. Consequently to gaze, hear, ponder, means something else, probably more related to the *sensus conformis*, the attitude to colouration of a time of recollection which Ignatius recommends in preparation for prayer.

   (vii) *Prayer of Images*
> A way of attempting an 'Ignatian Contemplation'. Take an Image and a Word from the scripture scene and submit to them. The Image and the Word must have some special quality of haunting, of reverberation in the spirit; they should evoke as it were an Ikon, not a pericope. For the Crucifixion the Image could be the Face of Christ described by Julian of

Norwich, or the face on the Turin Shroud; the Word, 'It is consummated... It is consummated... It is consummated...' For Bethlehem, the Image a star, the Word 'Glory to God...' The most obvious, the most adaptable, the most archetypal and the truest image of all is perhaps the Sacred Heart.

The Prayer of Images may be the most feasible way of doing an Ignatian Contemplation, for those who are used to praying. It has the advantage that a man opens himself to God's word rather than forcing his mind, and helps him be obedient to the rule, 'stay where you find what you want'.

(viii) *The 'Fool's Prayer'*

Take a very small passage of scripture, read a phrase, and slice it up finely. Repeat each 'slice' ten times or so, with a Name and a Remark. The Name with the in-breath, the Remark with the out-breath. End each 'decade' with a *Glory be*.

For example: The *passage*, Jn 1:1. The *phrase*, 'In the beginning'. The *slice*, 'Infinite God, how great you are', adapted to 'Lord, I praise you'; say ten times, 'Lord' on the in-breath, 'I praise you' on the out-breath. *Phrase*, 'was the Word'. *Slice*, 'Father, speak'; or Jesus, I hear'. Each ten times or so, ending with *'Glory be...'*

You see how slow all this is. We haven't got to the first comma yet, but for five minutes could have been soaking ourselves in scripture. It is called the Fool's Prayer because any fool can do it.

(ix) *Scripture 'bombing'*

A way of allowing God's word to break through the crust of our souls, to detonate inside; to impregnate us, while we remain passive. Read a verse, or perhaps two or even three, very slowly. Pause for sixty seconds. Read again. Pause. Thus for five readings. Then silence for as long as you can. Avoid all deliberate holy thoughts, all considerations and all activity between the readings – all that is deliberate and contrived – as far as possible.

4. *Methods – primarily for 'arid contemplation'*

In dry prayer, one wonders if one is doing anything at all. One is; but these 'methods' may give reassurance if used from time to time.

(i) *The Breathing Method* (St Ignatius' 'Rhythm Method' or 'Third Method of Prayer').

As far as I know this is the only traditional method of prayer in the Western Church which uses the breathing.

After reverent 'entry into God's presence' note is taken of the pace or rhythm of the breathing, taking care not to hold the breath or alter the pace. Then a vocal prayer is taken (Our Father, Hail Mary, Glory be, Soul of My Saviour etc.) and *with each in-breath one word is said.* I do not concentrate on the word, I do not think holy thoughts. I just do the drill. Surprisingly, it works for most people. What works? The heart, will, is able to rest in God. Why? Because the unwanted thoughts and the boredom are squeezed out of the mind which is wholly occupied in the very unintellectual activity of sending the words out. This takes more concentration than one would imagine – but it is concentration of a very simple kind. Any fool can do it; but by doing it he can be sure that each word and each breath is an act of love of God. From the words too a 'scent' of prayer arises higher in the soul, which can rest more easily in God.

There is a difference in attitude if the words are said on the out-breaths. Both ways are worth trying. Ignatius envisages such a prayer being made for an hour – perhaps twenty times round the Our Father. Like all practical things one can argue endlessly *a priori* whether it will work, but the way to find out is to try.

(ii) *The Jesus Prayer*

This is a prayer of the Eastern Church. Archbishop Bloom's excellent books usually describe it, and the classic *Way of a Pilgrim* is now in paperback from S.C.M. These explain the background and elements of the prayer. The most practical method for the non-adept Western Christian is to say it phrase by phrase with the out-breaths.

Two forms seem to be used, and fraternal piety suggests one should use the same formulae as our Eastern brothers:

'Lord Jesus Christ / have mercy on me;'

or

'Lord Jesus Christ / Son of God / have mercy on me / a sinner.'

The Jesus Prayer can be an appropriate way of 'informal prayer' also (cf. Appendix 1 para. 1). Like the Breathing Method, one can only tell if it will help by trying it.

(iii) *Deep Recollection*

The saints and mystics speak of 'leaving the senses behind' and 'going within' in prayer as something we must strive to do, and not merely as a process God can initiate. What they mean can be translated: 'As far as possible prescind from the distractions thrown up by your body and its senses, your imagination and intellect.' In this way we can hopefully attend to the presence of 'the Kingdom of Heaven within' which they recommend us to find. Their advice is therefore not platonic, dualistic, anti-matter; they are simply telling us to use our body and our minds in such a way that they help us attend to God's presence. There is no gimmick here, and no arcane spiritual ascesis. We use flowers, music, singing, silence as helps in prayer – here we use our bodies.

First, I picture my real, physical heart, gently concentrate on it, put my attention on it. This is easily done; one can concentrate on a part of one's body and after a while one begins even to feel it. The effect of concentrating on the heart is to get the thinking 'out of the head'; the brain does not hold the heart, but vice versa. As long as the thinking, such as it is, is of the heart, and as it were happening in the heart, distractions are absent. One has pulled oneself down below the surface thoughts, the waves on the sea, to the ground-swell beneath – the deep set of one's mind.

To get right down below that to the fine point of the soul, the place where Christ most truly is, is not possible – but one in some sense can pull oneself down a good deal deeper. From picturing my real heart, I turn it into a symbol: I make it a thousand miles wide and a thousand miles deep (still in the place of my heart though, not in my head!) And there, in the middle, I hold one very simple attitude before God. I hold the word 'Jesus'; or 'Lord'; or 'Mercy'; or 'Glory'; or 'Love'; or 'Blessed Trinity'; or 'Father'; or 'Holy'; or 'Sacred Heart'; or any word or short phrase I like. This holding can easily be done by saying the word in time with the breathing as described above.

The word or phrase used will obviously dictate the slant of

the prayer, which can be adapted to a Christocentric or Trinitarian approach (cf. chapter 2 no. 6).

What is being done in this method is to set up the psychosomatic mechanism, by drill and by numbers, in aridity, to be in the same stance that it finds itself when God does intervene in prayer. What a man does automatically and in reverent joy when God touches, is here done coldly and of set purpose. The object is not to squeeze a sensation out of God, which would be indecent even if it were possible, it is only to line the organism up in such a way that no barriers exist; it is to revisit the place God once visited; even, 'to go to the place one last found God'.

Or I could in slow stillness imagine the *dark things* in me falling away, and Christ (standing behind me, *smiling down at me*) laying his hands on my head and letting me draw his peace and light into my heart. This much would be 'recollection', a preparation for the praying – in which imagination will play no part.

For further reading: *Praying in Silence: an introduction to Centering Prayer* by John Jay Hughes (CTS D 539).

(iv) *Prayer by mediators*

In the *Spiritual Diary* of Ignatius it is likely that in places we see him 'making a colloquy'. When he recommends this in the *Exercises* he does not mean it as a work of the imagination or the intellect; it is far more sensitive and spiritual than that. It is probably a matter of being in actual, sensed contact with the 'mediator', as he describes the person prayed to. For us, in prayer where God does not intervene, it is a question of our opening ourselves to the mediator so that we may be taken over by him and led on higher. The term 'mediator' is obviously not applied univocally; for Ignatius the mediators are Our Lady and Our Lord; for us, it is well, as St Therese of Lisieux, did before Communion, to begin lower down, with the saints.

I pick a favourite saint to whom I have a genuine devotion, or at least a real attraction. I ask him to take my prayer over, actually to intervene, to manipulate my spirit. 'Great Saint, you are deputed by the Church to be an example, an intercessor, a mediator. And you and I have a special relationship of some sort. Now, please, take my prayer over. As of right I call on you, and ask you to hold me now before God as you are yourself.' I put myself in the same stance before God which I feel the saint has. I know how that saint looked on God when on earth; he is the same now. I set my heart as his was, and ask him to take over.

When nothing more seems to be happening, I go higher. With greatest reverence and supported by my saint I go to the Mother of God. Note well, this is not an exercise of imagination or thinking; with the saint to help, one is in very truth open to the touch of Our Lady.

After attending to her, taking all the time one wants, comes the next step. I ask Mary to do her office. Supported by her, and with the saint still with me, I let her turn me to her Son. Here, immense reverence. Before opening myself to Him, perhaps a slow recapitulation of Who and What he is: 'You are my God; my Creator (and I have rejected you); my King (and I a rebel); my Saviour (and so I look you in the face); my Redeemer (you value me so highly); my Brother (same Father, same Mother — you and I); my Food; my Life (you live in me, I in you)'. Then: 'Now, Lord, since this is so, I beg you to hold me, together with your Mother and my saint, before your Father'. Eventually: 'Holy Spirit, carry Christ's prayer from me to the Father. Now, face to face and as your Son I say "Father"'. It will be noted that much of this prayer can be looked on as an extended method of preparatory recollection. Obviously other 'mediators' can be added. There seems no reason why a living person — one very close to God and dear to oneself — should not be used to start the prayer, though here it is largely a matter of imagination and the relationship in the prayer may be 'of reason' rather than 'real'. Then a dead person could be approached — a relation, perhaps, who after all still belongs to one; then one's guardian angel, with whom a true involvement can be started after only a few days of this prayer; and then to the saint.

As in all prayer, the rule is 'stay where you find what you want'.

Again I emphasise; one is in touch with the mediator in fact, not in imagination; one must expect to be moved: one must be passive, and not keep talking.

(v) *Recollection by mood*

Teresa in *The Way of Perfection* hints at this. The principle again is to let the body help and not hinder. Suppose one is faced with an hour of prayer before breakfast, a splitting headache, a ghastly day ahead, too little sleep behind, and a stomach clamouring for a cup of tea.

'Lord I am useless this morning. I have a headache – so I turn to you with your crown of thorns. I dread today – you were faced with Good Friday. I'm half asleep – you were half dead. I need a cup of tea – you weren't going to get more than gall and vinegar. Your prayer then must have been even less "efficient" than mine is now! So – take me as I am; and suffer my aches and pains with me. I am only going to submit to my bodily state, and let you hold me before the Father.'

Any state of mind or body can be appropriate to some event or other of our Lord's life and set the scene for reverent awareness of God.

Five:

Formal Private Prayer:
A Defence

Let us not exalt prayer unduly. What is important in life is to do God's will; prayer itself is only valuable when and if it is God's will; it is for most Christians a means, not an end in itself; love of God, and therefore of men, has the primacy. Therefore it can be asked, Does God want prayer? These days perhaps more than ever before that question is often being answered negatively.

One way of effectively denying the need for prayer is to say that all a man's good actions are a prayer. Of course, if one defines prayer as 'anything done for God', then one might hope, optimistically, that statement to be true. But in fact such a definition is so wide as to be meaningless; prayer in the sense intended should be defined rather as *'explicitly adverting to God with reverence'*.

Is such a prayer desired by God? The Psalms, part of the very revelation of God and his Word, are all prayer. Our Lord himself was ever attentive to the Father and explicitly set aside time to pray (his contact with the Father at every moment did not excuse him from leaving works for prayer – rather it impelled him to do so). Our Lord too taught his followers to pray, told them to pray, told them to pray moreover outside the time of synagogue and Temple liturgy as well as inside it. Throughout the ages the closest followers of God, the saints, have without exception been men of prayer. Beyond the Christian religions, the wisest and the best of men have known that contact with the divinity is both possible and obligatory. One might guess moreover that man is by his very nature a contemplative animal, that when faced by beauty and splendour and goodness he will be compelled to be still and attend to it. For these reasons it would seem that rejection of private prayer is likely to be disastrous, and that those who speak against it or imply that it can be substituted by anything else have the onus of proof on them.

At the same time, it can be readily admitted that if there is a 'primacy of honour' in prayer, then that primacy belongs to the liturgy or to prayer in common. Such prayer is the prayer of the community, of the Body of Christ, while private prayer – likely though it is to be more personally rewarding than public prayer – is not only harder to be faithful to, and a very real mortification, but is essentially a humbler and more lowly action of the Christian.

Nevertheless one may well ask how much of oneself can be brought to the public prayer of the Church, and how totally one can hope to be present at the Mass, if there is no element of private prayer to support the action. It is unlikely that a man effectively participates in the action of Calvary and of the Resurrection (which is what the Mass is) if God does not force him, one way or another, to his knees at other times.

How much prayer should I do? Let us remember that those closest to God, the saints, were usually people who prayed much. Moreover, in these present days we are unlikely to *over*-estimate the need for prayer. I am inclined to think that we should, most of us, calculate the amount we feel we could and should do, and then double it. Error by excess is unlikely. Every voice today urges us to activity and 'relevance', little chance is there of our neglecting that particular truth. Of course, what God wants of us differs from person to person – there can hardly be a fixed rule for all. Still, if one truly desires to do the will of God, (and this is the purpose of life, the meaning of love of God, our joy and our duty) then one must be attuned to God, attentive to him, with the knowledge that comes from true and effective contact. Note too, that if God has ever given us 'consolations' in prayer, or a hunger for prayer, then we have experienced his invitation. To be quite concrete, if a man succeeds in reading this dry booklet, he can take it that God is asking him to lead a serious life of prayer.

Prayer has been defined as 'explicitly adverting to God with reverence.' Often enough, and it is a sign of the poverty of much of our approach to God, prayer is taken as being nothing except asking God for things, as if love between two people could be nothing except constant petition on the part of one, and of giving on the part of the other. If the petitioner is five years old this state of affairs can be tolerated, but not otherwise. Perhaps much of the ordinary Catholic's trouble with prayer is that he tries at the age of sixty to keep praying the way he did when he was six. Even if vocal prayer is used (and it does for many people form the bulk of their prayer – quite wrongly, I believe) the prayers are used often enough as so many little bribes, or like a strip of green shield stamps to purchase something from God. Now there is no doubt that prayer of petition in one way or another is essential, one has only to see Christ's insistence on it; but it can hardly be the heart of prayer.

Surely the heart and centre of our prayer must be the same as that of Christ, the prayer of the Son in whom we face the Father; and it must be the response of love. 'You are wonderful' is the love-response, and where God is concerned, it means Adoration. Not 'You are wonderful *for me*', even; nor 'Please give'; but 'You, in yourself, for what you are, demand my acclamation'. Gratitude is near to it. The Son is able to adore the Father only because he receives himself from him. Petition is not ruled out: 'Help me to respond!' (In the Blessed Trinity one could speak of the Son's demand *to be* as equal in efficacy to the Father's thought in generating.) Then for man, the love-response will mean that contrition or reparation will not be far distant. As has been said in chapter 4, these four elements, Adoration, Thanksgiving, Petition and Contrition/Reparation are classically the four 'Ends' for which Mass is offered; they are also the constituents of prayer; but it is always Adoration or Praise that is the centre and heart and which penetrates and informs the other three.

As to how one prays, there are some clear principles. First one must remember that it is Christ who prays, or in the case of a man out of the grace of God, then it is Christ who is drawing him and instigating the prayer. But if it is Christ who prays, then prayer is an act beyond and above our own capabilities. It is a supernatural act, a matter of God's gift. All we can do about it is, one way or another, to ask for the gift.

The asking for the gift of prayer must be sincere, one must truly want. This implies that to find God in prayer it is necessary to find him outside. Love is one; it is absurd to pretend to want to meet God in prayer when one has refused his will during the other hours. If there is one rule for 'successful' prayer, it is to love God. For most of us, failure in prayer is not due to ignorance of technique or to having the wrong thoughts, but rather to avoiding God's will in the rest of the day. Nor need our failure be concerned with something objectively serious; any willed, deliberate aversion to the known or suspected will of God will usually suffice to paralyse our prayer.

The asking too must be total. It need not be in words. One asks the same way that one communicates in other ways, by total expression. To ache before God is to ask. And the asking presupposes looking; we have to hunt for the prayer God wants of us, to experiment, to change, when things go badly; to follow one course when prayer is rewarded; to hold firm too when there is nothing in response and when we can see no plain source of infidelity on our part.

Prayer is often enough at once a necessity of our nature, a luxury and an agony. A necessity because we are made for God who is all beauty, and even here on earth the thought of him and of his touch should be obsessive; a luxury because if our lives are spent in his service we may be free to pray only rarely; an agony because we are built to desire God, but have made ourselves more or less incapable of experiencing him.

In this perplexity we must pattern our prayer on Christ's, whose it truly is. He is our approach to the Father, it is he who addresses God by name; and it is the Mass that is the pattern of his return as man to the Father. Here we have complete and total access to the Father because we are tied to, welded to, wedded into the Son in his return to the Father in obedience. We do not look much at Christ during the Mass, our eyes and hearts are towards the Father. As for Christ, effectively we and he are one. His Body, but we eat it and make it ours. His sacrifice, but we offer it; his presence, but our union together is the condition for it; our delegate consecrates, but it is Christ's body. He is too close to see, he is the action we do; our prayer is Christ's, is one of the ways he today prays to the Father. For that reason the motive and intent of the prayer cannot but be patterned on the redemptive movement of Christ.

Of course we can pray to our Lord as well as in him. To disbelieve that he was fit to be adored would be to deny that he was God. Indeed, he has to demand this worship from us. But because to pray to Jesus is the child's first prayer, we must not think that it is the only prayer for a Christian.

And what if I cannot pray 'in Christ'? What if I am separated from his Body in some sense by serious sin? Sinners too can want God. This said, it remains a fact that the first and essential characteristic of the Christian is that he is, or is meant to be, 'in Christ'. 'He has blessed us *in Christ* with every spiritual blessing ... he chose us *in him* before the foundation of the world that we should be holy and blameless before him' (Eph. 1:3,4). This situation of ours in the incarnate Second Person of the Trinity has its ramifications in every area of life: to live coherently at all will require a total, near-continuous assent to the fact of our being 'other Christs'.

In prayer therefore we are entitled to speak with his Spirit, or rather we are confidently to expect that the Spirit will demand to speak through us. 'God has sent the Spirit of his Son into our hearts crying "Abba! Father!"' (Gal.4:6). Such an assent of our whole person to sonship is 'The spirit *himself* bearing witness *with our spirit* that we are children of God' (Rom.8:15). Inevitably therefore our prayer should 'work' if it is petitionary, as effectively as Christ's own prayer, if we are truly with him.

Six:

Group Prayer

1. *The Principle, and a Definition*

Our Lord said 'Where two or three are gathered together in my
name, I am in the midst' (Mt.18:20). It would seem therefore that a
group of people who meet together, conscious of our Lord and
eager to do his will, are likely to find not only friendship, union,
support, but also – if he wills it – a special presence of Christ,
perhaps mediated through the companionship. It is reasonable to
suppose that some style of prayer could afford experience of this
fact, be a response to this specific presence. Let us call it Group
Prayer.

Any group of people praying together in the name of Jesus can
expect him to be present in their midst, as he promised. This would
apply to a congregation carrying out a liturgical act, and no less to
a family saying the rosary. But normally a congregation in a
church, or a family saying the rosary, would not advert to that
special presence. They are therefore not engaged in 'group prayer'
in the sense described above. But a group of people who con-
sciously intend to open themselves to that special presence are
engaged in group prayer, even though they are praying in silence.

Group Prayer can be defined as prayer with others, silent or
aloud, outside the Church's official Liturgy, where those praying
opened themselves to awareness of 'Jesus in the midst'.

2. *Recent antecedents of Group Prayer*

Inside the Church

    (i) Fr Lombardi's *Retreats of the Christian Community* (for-
merly 'Movement for a Better World').

    (ii) *Focolare* (a movement whose spirituality can be said to be
based on 'Jesus in the midst').

    (iii) *Cursillo* (a type of intensive group retreat).

Outside the Church
- (iv) *Moral Rearmament* (M.R.A.), formerly the 'Oxford Movement', started by Frank Buchman and later led by Peter Howard. One of the essentials was 'sharing'.

- (v) *Quaker Prayer* would seem to share some characteristics of 'Group Prayer'.

Outside Christianity
- (vi) *Alcoholics Anonymous* (A.A.) has Christian inspiration but manifests the strength and power of a group of people who may have only natural bonds.

- (vii) *Group Dynamics, Group Therapy*, and techniques associated, are more recent phenomena.

- (viii) A social climate of group-centredness, and a campus-philosophy with terms like 'I-thou', 'person-centred', 'God is other people', and where to be alone is horror, prepares a person for a certain amount of aberration – but also for Group Prayer.

3. *Pentecostal and Charismatic Prayer*

This is a significant development in Catholic spirituality in recent years. In this style of prayer it is awareness in some sense of the Spirit, not precisely of 'Jesus in the midst', which dictates the approach. However, since a group of people – sometimes a large number – is the normal occasion for Pentecostal or Charismatic prayer, and is usually a necessary condition for the reception of the 'gifts' or 'baptism of the Spirit', and since the Spirit is, after all Christ's, it is fair to classify it as 'Group Prayer' in the sense described.

A good book is *Did you receive the Spirit?* Tugwell, S., O.P. Pentecostal Prayer has devoted adherents, a few opponents who have been dismayed and some still suspicious onlookers. It plainly brings many people to God, supports many in a life of prayer and evidently has been the occasion for most remarkable phenomena. It does seem to have the disadvantage that some people who are not incapable of praying with others would nevertheless be permanently repulsed by the idea of speaking in tongues or singing alone in a room full of people or of asking for hands to be laid on . . .Such people might be misguided, might have to learn to adapt, but their position is understandable.

There does seem a case for a form of Group Prayer other than Pentecostal or Charismatic, if only as an introduction, for beginners, to higher things.

4. *Other Forms of Group Prayer*

(i) *Revision of Life* is an exercise used in some Religious Congregations, which does something of the job of the old 'Chapter of Faults'. It would best be essentially Group Prayer, if it is to succeed.

(ii) *Sharing the Word* is a way of using the Bible together. If it is not merely to be study or discussion, it would have to be prayer.

(iii) Near the threshold of Group Prayer is, or would profitably be, the *Gospel Enquiry* and *Social Enquiry* traditional in Catholic Action.

(iv) *Community Discernment.* Frs Futtrell and Toner S.J. have devised schemes for this on Ignatian principles. Their work is at present not widely available.

(v) '*Group Prayer*' in the sense used from now on denotes a structured form of praying together. There are as many methods of Group Prayer or Shared Prayer as there are groups of people praying.

5. *The Act of Faith in Christ's presence in the midst*

This is all important. If Christ is known by all to be present, and they act accordingly, then all that happens will be prayer. If they don't, the prayer group remains a group of embarrassed people sitting in a circle. The difference is between, shall we say, experiencing the Kingdom of Heaven established, and experiencing an abortive session of group dynamics.

If the act of faith is made not only will the meeting be 'safe', but various minor hazards will be avoided: people will not speak at too great a length, they will be honest, they will not sermonise or speak pietistically – all this sort of thing shrivels on the lips when we know Christ is present.

The implications of Christ's presence can involve this train of thought:

'If Christ is here, and glad to be – then I am glad. If he loves these people, then they are by definition my friends.'

'Further, they are Sacraments to me: it is because they are here that I have this access to Christ.

'If he is here, nothing could be said, done or even thought which would be unfit for his presence. Nothing false, contrived, artificial. Above all, nothing that would hurt or shock anybody else – nothing that would bring a frown to Christ's face.'

'If I could see Christ now, would I want to say anything – out loud before him and before these other people? If so, I will say it.'

'If I could see Christ and he caught my eye, would he want me to say whatever is passing through my mind and my heart? If he were to look at me, would he nod, say, 'Go on, say it'? If he would I will.'

'What, if anything, would he want me to say?'

'When anyone else says anything, I must bend over backwards to listen to it, to put a good construction on it – for he says it in Christ's presence, inspired by him.'

6. *Structure and Method in Group Prayer*

The Act of Faith in Christ's presence is all important.

There should never be any obligation to speak.

If the presence of 'Jesus in the midst' does not at any time help someone to pray, he can advert to other 'presences' – God present in his Word, in other individuals, in himself.

A chairman can be useful, because a strongly structured group will avoid the hazards and tears and bloodshed of group dynamics. The meeting begins and ends on time. There are 'rubrics'. When people are acclimatised and feel safe, say after three or four meetings, the structures and the rubrics can be allowed to dissolve.

The best setting is informal – in a living room, the chairs in a circle. Participants sit or kneel or squat. The numbers can conveniently be between three and fifteen.

The chairman's main task is to insist on the presence of Christ at the beginning, and if ever the sense of it is lost, to recall it: 'I think we are losing the sense of Christ's presence; let's recall it by three minutes' silent prayer.'

7. Benefits from Group Prayer

If the 'rules' of the prayer are adhered to – that is, that all assent to Christ's presence and act accordingly – it would seem impossible that anything embarrassing, awkward or painful could result. What normally happens is that the group of people not only find a helpful way of praying together but in addition find a sense of unity, of togetherness and mutual sympathy. All this should be regarded as a by-product. As soon as a group meets in order to experience mutual warmth and to meet each other, not only does the prayer tend to go but the warmth and the meeting goes too. If one looks for God, everything else follows; use God as a means to something else, and one is left with nothing.

There are of course natural reasons for the warmth, unity and peace which are usually experienced. These things occur presumably as results of psychological causes which operate in a group of people who are open and sensitive to each other. But grace normally operates in and through 'nature', and a sacramental religion finds nothing to be ashamed of in using a fitting 'sign' as a vehicle of grace. It is not a gimmick to use Ikons, holy water, organ music, stained glass, flowers, plainchant; nor can it be improper to use the most powerful sacramental of all – union with my brother – as a way of meeting Christ.

Prayer together brings permanent results. To meet others so closely, to be able (at last!) to talk together about what one really feels, to open oneself to God and to them, to see a little way into their hearts as they respond to God, to be able to speak to God with others supporting – this is to meet at a deep level. It is difficult to keep a quarrel going with men among whom one has found God, difficult to know others deeply and not to love them. With Group Prayer the Sermon on the Mount begins to look feasible.

Perhaps this is why so many religious welcome it. They, after all, claim to be establishing the Kingdom – they are the eschatological witness; they have left all things to follow our Lord and live according to his best advice, the counsels and the Sermon on the Mount. Obviously therefore they are likely to delight to set up the conditions for doing this and to be able to experience just for once the reality behind their life. But Group Prayer is not just for religious. Nor is it only for children at school. Adult lay people find this a valid way of prayer, and it is easy to see why: a structure of prayer enters their life, a way of learning to pray, an encouragement to taking up private prayer.

Three possible formats for Group Prayer are offered in Appendix 2. Group Prayer depends so much on the group; even, perhaps, on the 'chairman'. The formats therefore are provided only as a source of possible ideas – not as strait-jackets.

Seven:

Prayer through Sacramentals

1. *What Sacramentals are*

Vatican II defines Sacramentals as 'sacred signs which bear a resemblance to the Sacraments; they signify effects, particularly of a spiritual kind, which are obtained through the Church's intercession. By them men are disposed to receive the chief effect of the Sacraments, and various occasions in life are rendered holy.' It goes on to say: 'the liturgy of the Sacraments and Sacramentals sanctifies almost every event in men's lives ... there is hardly any proper use of material things which cannot thus be directed towards the sanctification of men and the praise of God.' (*Constitution on the Liturgy*, CTS Do 386, n. 60, 61.)

2. *How they work*

A wife who loses a child treasures a snapshot of it, or a toy it loved. She feels there is a sort of contact through the thing to the person – something more powerful and moving than a mere reminder. The Sacramental of a relic of the True Cross should do at least the same for any Christian. But in fact there is more to it than that: there really is a 'presence' of some sort.

The way Sacramentals work can be identified as an extension of the principle of Sacraments: a material thing, touched by Christ through the Church, becomes not only holy in itself but spiritually active for those who use it rightly. Men certainly hunger for signs, tokens, assurances, symbols, grace-laden actions. And from the Incarnation itself, downwards and outwards, even as far as the proper use of Lourdes water, God encourages the desire and the use.

3. *Sacramentals are pedagogically useful in the spiritual life*

It is a pity that too-spiritual Catholics do not agree with God about this capacity of material things, rightly used, to open us to grace. A sort of Gnostic snobbery can make people condemn what the Church praises. Of course, Sacramentals can be used superstitiously – but then so can Sacraments. The correct approach would be to teach the right use.

In nearly twenty years Liturgical Renewal has had no measurable effect on, say, the numbers attending Sunday or weekday Mass: perhaps the experts moved too fast, in spite of their good will. They tried to teach Liturgy before community was a fact; and they tried to teach active participation in the rites without building on what people actually knew and felt. Before teaching the Mass, they should have taught people how to kiss a crucifix, and why; before teaching how the Easter Vigil works, they should have taught how the Miraculous Medal works. If this sounds ridiculous, think it over: when a Catholic lapses from the faith, things slip in this order: Prayer, Confession, Communion, Mass, Marriage. The last things to go are – reverence for the Church and Priesthood ('Come in, Father. Will you have a cup of tea? I'm afraid we're not good Catholics, Father . . .') and – the Sacred Heart statue on the mantelpiece. A Catholic has to go very far before he throws that out (though today one finds religious people who through bad instruction have almost been taught to be iconoclasts). A reasonable pedagogy would have been to start from the small things people partially understand and value and thence lead them to the riches as yet unimagined.

4. *Prayer through Sacramentals*

If things can be 'touched by Christ through the Church' and thus become vehicles of grace, they become not only dear and precious but laden with, as it were, a certain potential activity of Christ. And if Christ is active, then he is 'present'. If he is present, it is ridiculous, if not sinful, not to attend. The way one attends is to use the object properly. There is a whole life of prayer open to us through Sacramentals, a whole mysticism. It stretches from the heart of the Sacred Liturgy itself down to the furthest ripple of the Church's prayer.

For the purposes of discussing prayer associated with Sacramentals, the term will be confined to Objects, not Actions; but it can be extended to comprise not only what the Church blesses, but what the Christian-in-a-state-of-grace touches: not only is the

Blessed Sacrament spiritually 'alive' but every brick laid by a Christian bricklayer is holy – and his building lasts in some sense, in God's eyes, for all eternity.

Sacramentals are a link between the prayer of liturgy and the prayer of finding God in all things.

5. *Examples of the spiritual mechanics*

(i) *Palms blessed on Palm Sunday*

'At the end of it all we take our palms home, and reverently place them behind our crucifix; and we would do well to use the palms of all the members of our family, placing them in the living room, the kitchen, the bedrooms, the garden – in any place where we pass our time – that they may remain there throughout the year. Why should we do that? Because when those palms were blessed, the priest said over them this prayer: "Bless, O Lord, these branches of palm and of olive which Thy servants receive in faith to the honour of thy name; so that those who dwell in any place where they are brought may obtain thy blessing. May all hostile influences be driven away, and may thy right hand protect those who have been redeemed by Our Lord Jesus Christ thy Son."

'The palms are not instruments of magic; they are not like superstitious amulets supposed to possess any power or virtue of their own; but they are the visible signs of the powerful prayer of God's Church which calls down the blessing of God upon all places where they are put. We who have faith in the Church should have faith in her prayers, and make use of their power to our sanctification and protection' ('*Preparing for Easter*, C. Howell, S.J., Burns Oates, 1955, pp. 68, 69.)

(ii) *Ikons*

A bit of wood is blessed, and thus 'touched by Christ'; various pigments are blessed; the paint brushes are blessed; someone in a state of grace (indwelt by God) and normally a Monk (consecrated by the Church to fulfil a charism as 'prophet' and 'apostle', which underlines the situation), while praying (and in direct contact with God) then paints a picture on the wood of Christ, Our Lady, or one of the saints. It is then solemnly blessed and dedicated after being led in procession to the Church.

The resultant artefact is highly charged spiritually. Used rightly it is not inert. And if such a thought seems barbaric and primitive, remember that the Church at the Second Council of Nicea in 787 upheld the veneration of images as giving a real connection with the person represented. We give the image 'relative worship', because the Ikon relates us to the person represented. An Ikonostasis hides the congregation from most of the Sacred Mysteries and from all the sanctuary – but it does not separate the Eastern Christian from the Liturgy of Heaven; on the contrary, it helps him 'actively participate'.

The Church orders that the images should be treated with the same honour with which we treat the Book of God's Word: lights, incense, the lot. And, a remarkable thought, it is for the same reason.

The way an Eastern Christian treats an Ikon is interesting: a candle is lit, and often, the image is touched or kissed: the Christian heart is saying 'Lord, I am touching and kissing this picture of your Mother: please make it be that I am *really*, spiritually, as close to her as I am physically to her picture. Mary, if I could see you instead of your picture, I would kiss you.' And here is the point – because of the Church's prayer God leans out of heaven and says 'Yes; as you want it, I *make it so.*'

The Sacramental then is an occasion of responding to a presence of Christ. The right response, in faith and with proper use, is a style of prayer appropriate to an activity or presence of Christ with which the object has been endowed by the Church's prayer.

6. *Sacramentals found in Churches*

To a Catholic open to this style of spirituality, holy things clamour. It ought to be impossible for him to step into a Church without being immersed in this sort of subliminal prayer:

(i) *The building:* 'Lord, as I enter here, I want you to take it as a prayer that I should enter heaven too.'

(ii) *Holy Water:* 'As I take this Holy Water I mean it, Lord, as a prayer of gratitude for my Baptism; and of petition that I be cleansed from my sins; protected from the devil; kept pure and healthy in soul and body; made fecund by your Holy Spirit' (cf. Ritual – Prayers for Blessing of Holy Water). 'By the Sign of the Cross I make a public profession of my gratitude to Christ for his Passion, my sorrow for what my sins did, my allegiance to Christ, and I invoke the Blessed Trinity.'

(iii) *Genuflection:* 'Jesus, I publicly profess my belief in your real Presence in the Tabernacle, Body and Soul as well as Divinity, and I adore you.'

(iv) *Statue of a Saint:* Here, the prayer operates on the same principles as with an Ikon. The 'honour' we give the object is termed 'relative', because it 'relates' us to the person depicted – truly and effectively if we use it in faith.

(v) *Candle before a Statue:* 'Lord, this candle is a sign of you, the Light of the world whom I greet. I use it as a prayer of petition that your light may shine in my life, and of gratitude for my Baptism. I use it to show I love this saint whose statue is before me. I want it to be a symbol of my prayer for as long as it burns.'

(vi) *Crucifix* (As for use of a statue).

(vii) *Stations of the Cross.* 'I would give a lot to go to the Holy Land, Lord. If I could, I'd walk to Calvary along the via dolorosa in Jerusalem – but I can't. But as I pass below these Stations, please bless me just the same.'

(viii) *Blessed Sacrament*

Not a Sacramental, of course, but *the* Sacrament. A presence of Christ in the most literal sense. It is what It is because of the Mass at which It was consecrated: presence before It is a reminder of, a thanking for, an asking for, a relative participation in the Mass. Properly taught, devotion to the Blessed Sacrament should open us to Mass-style and Trinitarian prayer.

(ix) *Relics*

The prayer here is valid in the same way as that before an

Ikon; the Western Church treats, or should treat, these as the equivalent. Today of course relics, and prayer through them, is often ridiculed, and presumably we will lose this good thing we have. But while the prayer is open to us, let us use it.

The theology of the relic, and to some extent the practical use (the Copts go to the extent of touch; they sit with cloth-wrapped relics and *cuddle* them) is that of the Ikon. Of course there is no liturgical blessing or consecration; the efficacy, the touch of Christ, has come a different way...

7. *Other Sacramentals in the home:*

(i) *Scapulars*

Let us not too readily mock the use of Scapulars. Look again at the Ritual's blessing. If one does feel inclined to ridicule the Brown Scapular, which gives a share in the merits of the Carmelites, it might be advisable for one single day of one's holiday to live the rule kept in an observant Carmelite monastery by a physically fit nun.

The Church tells us we can share in the merits of that sacrificial life without sharing its burdens, if we care to. The prayer element can be deduced easily enough.

(ii) *Lourdes Water*

A Sacramental only in an extended sense. What is meant by its use? 'Lord, as I use this water I praise you for your Mother: I thank her for all the graces given through Lourdes; I ask her help now, and that of St Bernadette; especially I ask for spiritual and physical healing; I offer my sufferings or difficulties in union with all others who love Lourdes and your Mother.'

(iii) *Medals:* 'Lord, as I put this miraculous medal in my son's pocket, I am asking you and your Mother to bless him. Let the presence of this medal on his body be a *symbol* of my continual prayer for him, which I would want to be unceasing. St Catherine Labouré, and all Saints and Blessed connect with St Vincent de Paul, please look to this.' If this seems superstitious, please read again Fr Howell's words quoted in paragraph 5, and see if this case is not analogous.

(iv) *Food*

While Grace after meals is a thank-you, Grace before is a blessing. That means that the food is sanctified. That means that if it is eaten in a Christian frame of mind, the meal *makes one holy* as well as, hopefully, enriching one's physical life. 'Lord, this food is your gift to my spirit as well as my body; and may the meal I share with others remind me of the union of love I owe to them.'

Eight:

The Sacrament of Penance as a Prayer-Style

1. *Confession brings a special 'presence' of Christ*

Each Sacrament is a moment when Christ touches, and therefore a moment when a man must respond to Christ. But a conscious response to the presence of God is prayer. Now in each Sacrament there is something remaining after Christ has touched – the 'Sacramental Grace'; something lasting, therefore, an attitude or a slant, could remain to colour our prayer.

In the Sacrament of Penance it could be put this way: we are commissioned by Christ to draw strength from our very weakness. Our prayer must reflect this.

What follows is a practical treatment of Confession designed to throw light on the 'prayer-style' appropriate.

2. *What Confession does*

Confession results in two main things. It gives God occasion to forgive sin, and this in turn gives special Sacramental Grace. The forgiveness of sin could happen in other ways; the Sacramental Grace is peculiar to Confession.

But there are other things that could, even *should*, happen. A book could be written about each: 'Indulgence', 'Cure' (not that we will ever not be tempted, but that we should be freed from slaveries), 'Humility', 'Spiritual Direction'. Let confessors note: 'Cure' may depend, under God, on *their* prayer and faith.

3. *The mechanism of forgiveness*

Forgiveness means that the sinner has repented and is welded to God in love again. The specific form the love takes is sorrow, or contrition. Now the return to love, the contrition, is God's gift; man for his part can supply an insufficient sorrow – 'attrition' – coward-sorrow, shame-sorrow; but love-sorrow, sorrow because of what sin did to Christ, the true sorrow of contrition, that is God's gift.

One may reasonably hope that such sorrow is given by God when one's heart turns to him in repentance. One may reasonably hope that the penitential rite of the Mass, or taking Holy Water, or any 'act of contrition' will effectively obtain the gift. One may reasonably hope that receiving Communion will do it – indeed the Church even asks us to be free even of the 'affection towards venial sin' before we go to Communion. In all these cases we may reasonably hope; but in Confession one *knows*, even if one does not feel. Why? The certainty is because this Sacrament, like the others, is a touch by Christ. Now when Christ touches, something happens: a blind man is touched by Christ, he gets his sight back: a deaf man is touched by Christ, he gets his hearing back; the woman with the issue of blood touches the hem of his garment, she gets cured after twelve years. Christ touches a leper, he gets cleansed; a paralytic, he walks. Christ touches a dead man, he is brought to life. Christ touches a sinner. . .? He gets his sins forgiven.

Now such is the mechanism of the Sacrament. Our sorrow may be insufficient – selfish, mean, cowardly; but it can be enough to get us to crawl to Christ. And if we touch him, then he puts into us perfect sorrow. You just cannot touch Christ, even with minimal faith, and leave the same way you came. The effect of Christ's touch in the Sacrament of Confession is, given the right conditions, to make the 'attrite' man who is insufficiently sorry truly 'contrite' with perfect love. A lack of feeling need not worry us. We *know* we are forgiven. It is not normal, after all, to feel grace.

4. *The mechanism of 'Sacramental Grace'*

Every Sacrament effects something more or less permanent. The permanent result is called the 'Character' in three Sacraments – Baptism, Confirmation, Orders; a 'quasi-permanent' result, called Sacramental Grace, occurs in the others.

The 'Character'-giving Sacraments happen once only because their work is done once and for all: the recipient has now been endowed with a permanently effective, infallible, call on God for the power to perform some office, though the grace may be rejected in certain ways. The other Sacraments also endow a man with a long-term effective call for help, but it is not necessarily life-long.

Two examples. In marriage a man and a woman receive Sacramental Grace which deputes them not just to afford and experience sexual pleasure, not just in doing so to express their love, not just — perhaps — in doing so to conceive new life: but in the very act to *make each other holy*. A Priest is deputed by God to 'make something holy' when he blesses it; in marriage, man and wife sanctify each other when they kiss. Their bodies have become vehicles of grace for each other.

In the Anointing of the Sick, again the recipient is endowed with a quasi-permanent 'vehicle of grace'. Suppose a man with cancer is anointed. That cancer is growing; cell by cell, inch by inch, it is squeezing the life out of him; in its wake it brings agony, and worse for the relatives. The man then has it touched by Christ in the anointing. Cell by cell, inch by inch, the thing goes on growing; but cell by cell, and inch by inch, just as it is squeezing his human life out of him so it is *conferring Christ's life*. And so it goes on, into the death agony, through the moment of death — the man is, in the very process of losing his own life, being endowed with Christ's.

What then can be the 'vehicle of grace', the quasi-permanent effect, the sacramental grace in Confession? It is the very weakness which gives rise to sin. The alcoholism, which has in the past, and could now, lead a man to sin, becomes potentially a permanent, powerful call on God's help; the very drug-addiction becomes a possible source of grace; the sex hang-up is now a deputation to praise God in a special way by resisting the temptation. Sin may still result, of course, Hell may result; one may refuse the grace. But the temptation, and more than the temptation, the very weakness which is perhaps the result of sin as well as the possible source of sin is now potentially an opening to Christ's life and to sanctification.

5. *How Confession 'works', and why we go*

Confession 'works', as has been said, because in the Sacrament one 'touches' Christ for forgiveness — and Christ has pledged himself to respond. But how do we touch Christ? By touching his Church, which is his Body. The way we touch the Church is by the seven Sacraments; and one of these is specially ordered for the forgiveness of sin.

That is why faiths of Catholic tradition (Roman, Anglo-, Coptic, Byzantine, Syrian etc.) have a Sacrament of Penance, and those of Protestant tradition do not: the former believe the Church is 'Body' in a way the latter do not. They do as Catholics do – tell God privately they are sorry for their sins. But Catholics, believing Christ is to be touched, do more: they make their sorrow 'incarnate' by going to where they know Christ is to be found, in the Church, and 'touching' Him.

The patron of Confession-goers is 'the woman who was a sinner' in Luke 7. She knew two facts; first, that she was a sinner; secondly, that Christ was to be found in the supper-room of Simon the Pharisee. Her grasp of these two facts resulted in her having to enter the room, go through the guests, throw herself at Christ's feet and kiss them. Knowledge of the same two facts results in the Catholic going to Confession. We would have mistrusted the women's sorrow if, knowing Christ was there, she had contented herself with telling God in her heart that she was sorry – and going on to do the shopping. Similarly one might mistrust the grasp a Catholic had of the two facts – his sinfulness and Christ's presence in the Church – if his sorrow was not externalised in 'touching Christ' in the Church, at least fairly frequently.

6. *The effect of forgiveness*

One aspect of the Sacrament has implications it is hard to accept, and gives a light so bright we can scarcely dare to see by it. It is that our sins are forgiven. God sees us guiltless. We are innocent. Well then, we must know the fact, and be accordingly glad. A man is as God sees him: if God says I am innocent then I am, and must live in the light of the fact.

What happens is that God the Father sees the whole of our life and, after Confession, he sees in it nothing that does not give him glory. There is nothing in it which does not shine up with splendour to him. Much of my life – all the time that I was in a state of grace and not actually sinning – gave him glory; that part was fine. But what of the moments of sin, especially of grave sin? Here is the beauty of it. Those moments have been touched by Christ; if mortal sin, it was his crucifixion that was required to effect redemption; venial sin too at least requires his Blood. This means that it is the moments of sin, which have been thus touched by Christ, which are, now, the most beautiful moments of my life. The Father sees my life before him, and he sees the moments of my sin as, above all others, shining up with beauty to him. This is no credit to us; we just sinned. The credit is Christ's. But the effect is that our whole life, and especially the moments of sin, are now glorious. After Confession, the whole of our life is a complete success story. We are free of the burden of the past. How blind those Catholics are who depreciate the value of Confession!

7. *The need of forgiveness*

We are sinners. We need saving. At least, it certainly looks as if Christ thought so. (One might try, too, asking our Lady at the foot of the Cross how seriously *she* takes sin; she watched him die.) The Passion is one result of sin; another could be damnation. Hell exists. (It must; given the fact that we will live for ever before God's face, and given the fact that, by free will, we have it in our power to self-mutilate ourselves spiritually and make ourselves incapable of enduring proximity to God. The pain of enduring Him would be hell.)

How bad is sin? We know what it cost Christ. How bad is it for us? In Mk 7:21-23 there is a list of things which make us 'unclean', ritually unfit to worship, filthy in God's eyes. Apart from the obvious things, covetousness, malice, deceit, lasciviousness, envy, pride and folly are mentioned. In that case the chances are there is plenty in me to make Christ think I need saving.

Isn't Christ rather hard? The difficulty is, he loves us. He can't tolerate in us things that are destroying us. He'd die to put it right. In fact, he did.

8. *Sensitivity to sin is healthy, not morbid*

If I have cancer, it's a good thing to know. If I need saving, it's a good thing to know (otherwise, might I not fail to recognise a Saviour?). Awareness of sin is in fact a correlative of awareness of God. You cannot possibly be close to someone whom you love without being aware of when you hurt them; it is mere insensitivity not to register these moments, an indication of grossness. So it is with us and God. The saints were vividly aware of their sinfulness precisely because they loved him so and were so close.

There comes a time when 'pre-evangelisation' must cease and God's word be preached; a time for evangelisation. God's mind and God's law has to be explained; as a consequence, one is invited to accept the fact of one's guilt or to reject it.

The Pharisees, and the mockers in Herod's palace on Good Friday, did not know they were sinners; Our Lord's attitude to the one group was insult and vituperation, to the other silence. Please God, we are not among them but among the motley throng of sinners who know they are such; Peter, the woman who was a sinner, the woman taken in adultery, Matthew. If we are, we will meet our Saviour.

9. *Frequent Confession*

If I know I am a sinner I will want to 'touch Christ' in repentance. I will want to open my deep need to him. I will want the Sacramental Grace as much as I want forgiveness; more perhaps, with 'venial' sin.

How often should one go to Confession? The Church's discipline in this Sacrament has changed vastly in the course of time; what we want to know is the mind of the Church today. One thing is clear: the Church's old obligation to go to Confession, with Communion, at 'Easter or thereabouts' is not an indication of the desirable frequency, it is simply a statement of the fact that one who, in mortal sin, neglects to do even this much has yet further insulted God by further grave sin.

The Church's mind can be inferred easily enough by its legislation.

(i) *Secular Priests:* the old canon law told Bishops to encourage their Priests to go weekly to Confession. In this context Vatican II advised Priests to go frequently.

(ii) *Religious:* In 1970 Rome asked Religious to go frequently and by frequently it specified fortnightly or weekly (S.C.R.S.I. Decree *Dum Canonicarum*, December 1970)

(iii) *'Lay people':* (here this term stands for non-Priests and non-Religious)
They too are called to 'perfection of charity'. Presumably, if they go to daily Mass and live a recognizable prayer-life, the Church would not wish them deprived of what it recom-

mends to Religious. A reasonable guess: fortnightly or weekly Confession.

If they are weekly Mass-goers, one could hazard the guess that twelve times a year is not inappropriate. Pope John Paul II said when he visited Ireland: 'It was with great joy that I received the news that the Irish Bishops had asked all the faithful to go to Confession as part of a great spiritual preparation for my visit to Ireland... You could not have given me a greater joy or a greater gift. And if today there is someone who is still hesitating, for one reason or another, please remember this: the person who knows how to acknowledge the truth of guilt, and also asks Christ for forgiveness, enhances his own human dignity and manifests spiritual greatness. I take this occasion to ask all of you to continue to hold this Sacrament of penance in special honour, for ever. Let all of us remember the words of Pius XII in regard to frequent Confession: "Not without the inspiration of the Holy Spirit was this practice introduced into the Church." '

10. *Difficulties about Confession – with short replies*

(i) 'I can't really be sorry, because I'm always telling the same sins.' A drug-addict, an alcoholic, can be sorry – truly sorry – even though his addiction makes him fall frequently.

(ii) 'I am embarrassed because I always tell the same sins.' Thank God they are not *new* sins! Would you be happier if you had a brand new sin to tell each time?

(iii) 'What will the Priest think?' Unless he is a fool, the bigger the sins are – and the longer you have been away – the more he will be in admiration of you, and gratitude to God.

(iv) 'I can't stand the Box.' Then ring the Presbytery bell and ask to see a Priest.

(v) 'I don't see the point of trotting out a shopping list.' Words are symbols; the words are inadequate to express your deep sinfulness – but they are enough for the Priest to do his job. God, whose absolution it is, can reach down to the reality far beneath the words. The words are only a sign – although a necessary one.

(vi) 'I feel I get nothing out of Confession.' Feelings do not matter very much; what one knows and what one does is important, not what one feels. Grace, union with God, is something normally deeper than feelings. At the same time, the Sacrament ought to comprise a significant 'sign'. The Penance Service outlined in Appendix 3 is designed to help here.

(vii) 'There is no spiritual direction in Confession.' A valid objection: there ought to be. But even without it, surely the Absolution and the Sacramental Grace make it worthwhile?

(viii) 'I don't know how to go to Confession any more; I don't know how to tell my sins.' So just say six words to the Priest: 'Father, help me to tell my sins.' Then the Priest will ask you all he needs to know – shortly and gently.

11. *Contrition and Examination of Conscience*

There are five main elements in Confession and if our Confessions seem unsatisfactory all we can do is to alter our practice of one or more of them.

(1) Absolution: no change needed here.

(2) Penance: we might try making our token penance into something larger – the Priest probably won't.

(3) The way we tell our sins: trying to make it interesting for the Priest, or trying to express motivation with accuracy, usually doesn't help. ... A bare list (of sins, not of psychological states) is as good a way as any, seeing that words, no matter how accurate, are but symbols.

(4) Examination of Conscience: most readers of this book are likely to have adequate self-knowledge. In Appendix 4 there is an Examination given which might be of use to teachers of others. Good headings are 'God', 'Other People', 'Things difficult to confess', 'Vows' (for religious), and – vital to look at if not to verbalise for the Priest – 'Roots of sin'.

(5) Contrition: it is here that we must make the alteration if we are dissatisfied with our Confessions. Fifteen minutes prayer on the Passion is probably the best act of contrition to aim at.

Nine:

The Problem of Prayer of Petition

A word has to be said about petitionary prayer, since scepticism on its value is a spiritual defect so radical that it raises a question about any form of prayer the subject might make. There are two problems; the philosophical one and the theological one.

1. *The philosophical problem about prayer of petition*

How can my prayer affect God's universe, since its future state is predetermined by its past? What good is it praying for fine weather tomorrow, when what is going to happen depends on a depression over the Azores a month ago, and a cold front over Iceland this afternoon? How is God going to alter it?

The problem is a false one. Only to a strict materialist is there a difficulty.

The materialist position is that nothing exists except matter, and the consequences of matter. Therefore all that happens is explicable only in terms of matter and its behaviour, and is – in principle – open to complete explanation in such terms.

But his position is false on two counts, and is in addition self-contradictory. Therefore a different position – a non-materialistic one – has to be maintained.

First, if everything that happens is totally explicable simply in terms of matter, it would follow that all that happens is predetermined so to happen according to the normal operations of matter. But if this is so, the workings of my brain too is predetermined, and I am bound, inexorably, by the immutable operations of my brain-cell chemistry and electricity, to be thinking exactly what I am thinking. And if this is so, what I take to be perception of truth could never be more than the response to a reflex; it is sheer illusion to think that one could *reason* to the perception of *truth*.

Consequently a materialist position fails to explain the innate certainty of 'it *must* be true; I *see* it is'. It fails to explain reason.

Secondly, it fails to explain the sense of obligation. If my sense of 'ought' is pre-determined its value is negated. A man's taste for sadistic murder is morally as neutral as his taste for gorgonzola. He is made like that. The *instinct* to praise or blame remains explicable of course, but there can be no meaning to praise or blame.

Thirdly, this position is contradictory. The materialist *reasons* to the conclusion that only matter exists; but if that is so, reasoning is false. He has proved that proofs are impossible. Also, his desire to argue his case ('I *must* explain this to them!'), his sense of obligation, is meaningless: even the basic fundamental premise 'I, and others, must accept truth' is empty of content. His position on two counts is self-contradictory.

On three counts therefore the materialist position fails. But if it is false that 'nothing exists except matter, and therefore nothing happens except the operations of matter,' then it must be true that 'something exists other than matter, and therefore the operations of matter do not explain everything.' The 'something other' we call spirit; it is intrinsically independent of matter.

To explain the validity of reason and of the sense of obligation, I must therefore postulate spirit. But if spirit is present in the operations of my brain cells (which operations can all be explained physically by the pre-existing physical, chemical and psychological states, which are all that can be detected in the laboratory), spirit can also be present enmeshed in the workings of the material universe outside my skull.

In short, I can and should pray for fine weather tomorrow if I want to. The creation of the world, the Crucifixion, the weather a thousand years ago, my prayer, and the weather tomorrow are all one action of God.

This abbreviated argument, too short, too slick, too slack, which is given above is best seen in C. S. Lewis's book *Miracles* (Fount paperbacks).

2. *The theological problem about prayer of petition*

'Believe me, you have only to make any request of the Father in my name, and he will grant it to you. Until now, you have not been making any requests in my name; make them, and they will be granted, to bring you gladness in full measure' (Jn 16: 23, 24).

'As long as you live on in me, and my words live on in you, you will be able to make what request you will, and have it granted' (Jn 15: 7).

Here is the problem of prayer of petition. Our Lord's words – and one can pick other passages – don't seem to be true.

We did ask the Father in his name; we didn't get what we asked for. We did ask with faith, and repeatedly (at least, the Church has), and it doesn't happen. What is wrong? Well obviously to 'ask in our Lord's name' is more than to use a form of words: it means 'to ask with Christ's authority'. Surely then, to ask in a state of grace must be to ask in Christ's name; or to ask at Mass? Surely one is *deputed* by Christ to ask then? Evidently not. Experience proves that such prayer is not necessarily answered.

Can one say that 'if two of you agree over any request that you make on earth, it will be granted them by my Father who is in heaven' means that union and love in the community is the source of authenticity in prayer and moreover to be the means by which the prayer is fulfilled. As if 'God-with-us', we ourselves, by discerning love, answer the needs of each other? Well, perhaps we might; but we won't cure the sick child in Lourdes or save the breaking home in Australia. From experience, that answer won't work either.

Then when *is* one deputed by Christ to ask in his name? Obviously, if I could hear our Lord whisper: 'quick, ask my Father for *that*', my request would be answered: If Christ asks for a thing, it is bound to happen; if he cares to ask through me, it is still bound to happen. The problem of prayer of petition resolves quite simply into a problem of discernment of spirits: is Christ telling me to ask for this thing or not? If he is, it's bound to happen.

Why should Christ work through us, get us to do his asking for him? Well, that is what we are for: we are his mystical body; we are the way – one of the ways, the normal way – in which he is present on this earth. Our hearts, our *free* will, to be the way he loves; our mouths to speak *his* words; our hands to do *his* work. Our prayer too is simply one of the ways he praises his Father, and asks. He sub-delegates *his* concerns to us.

Of course, if we were properly sensitive to Christ and able to detect when he wanted us to ask for things we would, like the saints, be working miracles. How did Philip Neri know that the boy would come back to life when he prayed over him? Simple: our Lord told him to ask. And how are we to learn sensitivity, learn when to ask? Probably by acting, sometimes, on hunch. The Spirit's movement can be eccentric, irregular; it cannot contradict the law, order, of Christ and the Church, but it can be original. To say *this* to this person; to read *that* book; to pray for *this* person or event; to do penance for *this* intention. Sometimes we will make mistakes, but trial and error might lead us to be able to distinguish the authentic flavour of the Good Spirit, the Voice of Christ. And sometimes, we might hit the jackpot.

Our task is to learn to find out when we are deputed by Christ to ask in his name.

Ten:

The Mass

1. *Importance.*

The Mass is not only the centre of our Faith, it is the moment when heaven penetrates this world and it makes us present − truly and in reality − to Christ as he was on Calvary and at the moment of the Resurrection.

The difficulty, of course, is that while we *know* this is true, we do not feel it. But as with so much of life, here too we have to disregard the unhelpful feelings and to live in the light of what we know. Of course if 'feelings' can help then we use them; and more and more since the renewal of the liturgy after Vatican II we have done our best to make active and intelligent participation in the mystery as possible as may be − even to children.

But it *is* a mystery. Canon 899 reminds us 'the Eucharist is an action of Christ himself and of the Church. In it Christ the Lord, through the ministry of the priest, offers himself, substantially present under the appearances of bread and wine, to God the Father . . .' Who could exhaust the meaning of that? Or the importance? And the Council speaks of the liturgy, more than once, as 'the summit toward which the activity of the Church is directed: it is also the fount from which all her power flows. For the goal of apostolic endeavour is that all who are made sons of God by faith and baptism should come together to praise God in the midst of his Church, to take part in the Sacrifice and to eat the Lord's Supper'. How can one comprehend what gives meaning to the whole of life − perhaps the whole of creation?

'Christ offers himself' . . . 'the fount of the Church's power' . . . perhaps the fullest and 'easiest' elaboration of this is available in the Pope's document *Dominicae Cenae* of 1980 (CTS); the shortest, clearest plea against abuses (which are many, varied, deeply injurious to unity and often indicative of radical ignorance of doctrine) is in *Inaestimabile Donum* of 1980 (CTS Do 522). The first part of this chapter seeks to 'explain' the Mass and to counter abuse.

2. *The essential insight*?

There are innumerable ways of looking at the Mass. What I give here is only one way. It leaves out clear emphasis on the community aspect; on the implications of the paschal meal; on ways of participating; and on much else. But it does pick out the essential. Please read carefully, several times, the next two paragraphs.

The night before he died Jesus Christ said, more or less: 'Listen, you who are my close friends: I tell you now that *THIS* (he points to the bread) is my Living Body; and *THIS* (he points to the wine), this is my Living Blood. Now, *DO THIS* (that plainly is an order) and every time you do − you will be present to my living Body and my living Blood *AS IT WILL BE FOR YOU TOMORROW, WHEN I DIE ON THE CROSS.'*

Jesus Christ, who is God, has thus devised a way of making what happened in history nearly two thousand years ago on Calvary happen . . . here! now! And *why* would he want us to be present with him at Calvary (present *in fact* that is, not present in imagination or through a sort of pious mime)? Well, two reasons come to mind very easily. First, companionship: he did not have many *friends* with him on Calvary − but at Mass he can have you and me! And that surely is a joy to Jesus Christ and to his Mother . . . But there is a second reason. If he can have you and me *really* with him at Calvary, when he returns to his Father ('. . . when he returns to his Father?' . . . present then also at the moment of the *Resurrection*) well then − *WE ARE SAVED!* The Mass really *is* the work of our Redemption: there is nothing more important, nothing more costly, nothing more beautiful. If we can be with him at Calvary, with him in the garden of the Resurrection (not just physically present, but willed to him, welded to him, wedded to him) then his work for us is achieved. Of course because we need to be with him at Calvary and the moment of the Resurrection (and of the Ascension, and of Pentecost . . . all that is involved in his return to his Father, in his Passover), and because we live in space and time, we need to reiterate our decision; Mass is not something we are to do just once.

3. *'Obligation'*

And that is the reason for the obligation to go to Mass on Sundays and days of Obligation. It is not that the Church is laying down a rule so much that she is making a statement of fact: "Look, either you believe what I say about the Mass, or you don't. If you don't believe, you have lost the Faith. If you do believe, and you cannot be bothered to go (not 52 times in the year, on the Lord's day, and a handful of other days) . . . well then, your heartlessness seems almost worse. Can't you see it's important?" That is what the Church means when it says "You've got to go to Mass on Sundays."

Notice that the Mass 'works' not because you and I are praying (though our prayer is a condition for receiving the gifts God wants to give) but because *CHRIST IS PRESENT*. The Mass is not a prayer service over a bit of Blessed bread − used as a symbol of our unity together and of the body of Christ; *THE LIVING CHRIST IS ACTUALLY AND ACTIVELY PRESENT*. (And it is *not* a bit of Blessed bread, it is Jesus in the moment of his return to his Father.)

It is knowledge of these facts that makes the Mass an addiction for the informed Catholic − the sweetest addiction there is. And of course, although a slovenly priest celebrating the Mass, or an irreverent liturgy, or banal music, or vacuous sermons, or a headache, or a million other things may be annoying (or even scandalous), they cannot destroy the value of the Mass. The Mass gives perfect glory to God, and perfect praise to the Father, because it is Christ's work. Neither you nor I, nor the Priest, can spoil it. And a good motive for going? . . . *What Jesus Christ gets out of it*; not what I get out of it. (And certainly not what I may *feel* I get out of it.)

4. *The 'shape'*

It can be useful, when taking part in the Mass, to keep in one's mind the basic structure. That way it is easier to recall one's wandering attention and, by opening oneself to the 'attitude' appropriate to that part of the Mass, resume a closer participation. (Sophisticated readers must here permit an elaboration of what is often taught to children.)

The Mass is in two parts − a Liturgy of the Word and a Liturgy of the Eucharist − with (as one may envisage it) a space in between. Each of these two parts has two movements: one 'up' to God and one 'down' from God. The whole becomes a sort of 'M' shape.

The Liturgy of the Word, at least on a Sunday, takes most of the time. Bordeom? Yes, if one does not know how to listen to God's Word, if one does not love the Bible, perhaps if one has not prayed the readings over beforehand, if one has not acquired the knack of

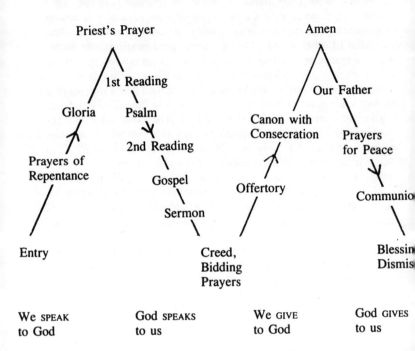

LITURGY OF THE WORD

Priest's Prayer

1st Reading

Gloria   Psalm

Prayers of
Repentance   2nd Reading

Gospel

Sermon

Entry

EUCHARISTIC LITURGY

Amen

Our Father

Canon with
Consecration   Prayers
for Peace

Offertory   Communio

Blessin
Dismis

Creed,
Bidding
Prayers

We SPEAK to God	God SPEAKS to us	We GIVE to God	God GIVES to us

prayer . . . Catholics who say they get bored at Mass are really saying
that their spiritual life is weak in these areas. (Of course, in the second
part of the Mass it would be impossible to be bored once one knew
what was happening, and providing one believed it).

5. *Union with God*

Those who cannot go to Communion, for *WHATEVER* reason, should
never feel it is not worth going to Mass. It is true the normal
consummation of our presence at Calvary and the moment of the
Resurrection, of our will to identify ourselves with Christ's gift of
himself to the Father, would be to go to Communion. There are

innumerable overtones to this action, and they must have been present — and must be present now — to the mind of Christ. There is the 'making of unity' with our fellow guests at the feast. The pledging ourselves to our Host, and the glad acceptance of his responsibilities towards us (one remembers the implications in the Middle East, even today, of having taken food and drink in someone's house). The union with not just the guests and the Host, but with the Victim; the being-built-into-Christ as well as the 'receiving' of what he has to give. The intended union with all God's people who celebrated the Pasch throughout the ages. The realisation that there are spousal and nuptial — frankly sexual-overtones: "the union I want with you", says Jesus, "I can only express by using food symbolism; I cannot use sexual symbolism as the pagan religions did, I will go beyond that and I will say to you, 'do not simply embrace Me, consume my Living Body and Blood.'" To put it simply: we give great joy to the Sacred Heart.

All this, of course, depends on the Real Presence. The Mass 'works' not because you and I are praying, but because Christ is truly present.

But the major 'work' in the Mass is in the movement 'we give to God'. We give, on Sunday, money . . . Money is work, skill, sweat, sacrifice — it is in a way a bit of one's self, one's life that one is giving. And it is in fact one's *whole* self one is meant to give — money or not, Sunday or not. One's prayers, works, actions, joys, sufferings; one's loves and cares; one's failures and sins; all the content of one's heart. Most of all, one's love. Active participation in the Mass (*actuosa participatio*) does not mean primarily movements or words — it means total, internal, willed, union with Christ's sacrifice: a process that begins long before I enter the church door.

All this gift of self is symbolised by bread and wine — which need so much work to produce. And something utterly wonderful happens to this bread and wine: God takes it over, and it becomes the Living Christ. And what you and I brought to Mass is swept up in Christ's action, and brought before the throne of the Father.

The Church always encourages prayer before the Blessed Sacrament. It is prayer before the Risen Christ in person, for the value of the Blessed Sacrament lies in the fact that It is what It is because of the Mass at which It was consecrated. Every aspect of the Eucharistic devotion can and should be a thanksgiving for the last Mass one was present at, and an anticipation of the next. Devotion to the Blessed Sacrament is normally commensurate with the understanding of the Mass; and if I want to love the Mass more, a good starting point would be to pray more — before the Blessed Sacrament.

Eleven:

The Rosary

1. *Why and How?*

The best reason for saying the rosary is that it is a way of penetrating prayerfully thirteen events of our Lord's life, and two aspects of the glorious life of heaven. An effective way for us to do this must obviously be something that our Lord wants us to know about and use. Perhaps this is why Our Lady is so anxious for it (implicitly she asked for it at Lourdes and − unless the Ordinary Magisterium has grossly misled us − quite explicitly she has asked us at Fatima); she must be glad when we do something which will lead us to her Son. With the encouragement the Church has always given to the saying of the rosary, and still does give, it is a perverse Catholic who would speak against it − and a foolish one.

Legend links the origin with St. Dominic, and Dominicans have certainly been its foremost propagators. Historically it grew with the desire for the laity to have 150 prayers to link them with the 150 psalms used in monastic prayer. There was long and intricate evolution which ended in the sixteenth century with the rosary as we have it − modified now by most people, unofficially but sensibly, with the optional addition of the 'Fatima prayer' after each 'Glory be'.

If one were beginning to say the rosary for the first time, one would do well to 'train' oneself by taking a mystery a day, preceded by a relevant bit of scripture (see 6 below), for fifteen days. After that one should know the mysteries and could start in with five mysteries a day.

2. *How it works.*

The rosary works at five levels. First, the sense of touch. Merely to finger the beads is an opening to prayer . . . for the beads have presumably been blessed, and a blessing is from the Church, the Body of Christ; so a blessed object has in some sense been touched by Christ, and the mere fingering of it should be an occasion of love.

Secondly, lips — the rhythmic repetition of the words. One is hardly expected to concentrate on the meaning of the words of the Hail Mary fifty times in succession in twenty minutes. But then the words do not have to be used for their intellectual content; their repetition, punctuated by the Holy Name, allows a 'scent' of prayer to rise to a higher level.

Thirdly, imagination; and fourthly, thinking. There is a picture to be held in the imagination and a lesson to be drawn by the mind. Not new ones each time, familiar ones. Perhaps only for one Hail Mary out of the ten will this be done, but at least for that space one has praised God with one's imagination and one's intellect.

But it is at the fifth level that the prayer is really happening. This is the level of contemplation, where the will (the loving faculty) hangs on to God. In a word, the rosary is a sophisticated device for aid to contemplation.

3. *The Prayers to know:*

The Sign of the Cross

In the name of the Father, ✠ and of the Son, and of the Holy Spirit. Amen.

The Apostles' Creed

I Believe in God, the Father Almighty, Creator of heaven and earth; and in Jesus Christ, his only Son, our Lord; who was conceived by the Holy Spirit, born of the Virgin Mary, suffered under Pontius Pilate, was crucified, dead and buried. He descended into hell; the third day he rose again from the dead; he ascended into heaven, and is seated at the right hand of God the Father Almighty; from thence he shall come to judge the living and the dead. I believe in the Holy Spirit, the Holy Catholic Church, the communion of Saints, the forgiveness of sins, the resurrection of the body, and life everlasting. Amen.

The Our Father

Our Father, who art in heaven, hallowed be Thy name. Thy kingdom come. Thy will be done on earth as it is in heaven. Give us this day our daily bread, and forgive us our trespasses as we forgive those who trespass against us. And lead us not into temptation, but deliver us from evil. Amen.

The Hail Mary

Hail Mary, full of grace, the Lord is with thee: blessed art thou among women, and blessed is the fruit of thy womb, Jesus. Holy Mary, Mother of God, pray for us sinners, now and at the hour of our death. Amen.

Glory be to the Father

Glory be to the Father, and to the Son, and to the Holy Spirit; as it was in the beginning, is now, and ever shall be, world without end. Amen.

The 'Fatima' Prayer

O Jesus, forgive us our sins, save us from the fire of Hell and lead all souls to heaven, especially those who have most need of your mercy.

(Note: this prayer is not an official part of the Rosary, but it is nowadays commonly said after each 'Glory be'.)

The Hail Holy Queen

Hail, holy Queen, Mother of Mercy, hail our life, our sweetness, and our hope! To thee do we cry, poor banished children of Eve; to thee do we send up our sighs, mourning and weeping in this vale of tears. Turn then, most gracious Advocate, thine eyes of mercy towards us; and after this our exile show unto us the blessed fruit of thy womb, Jesus. O clement, O loving, O sweet Virgin Mary.

V. Pray of us, O holy Mother of God.

R. That we may be made worthy of the promises of Christ.

The Rosary Prayer

Let us pray:

O God, whose only begotten Son, by His life, death, and resurrection, has purchased for us the rewards of eternal life; grant, we beseech Thee, that meditating upon these mysteries in the most Holy Rosary of the Blessed Virgin Mary, we may imitate what they contain, and obtain what they promise: through the same Jesus Christ our Lord. Amen.

4. *The use of the Beads.*

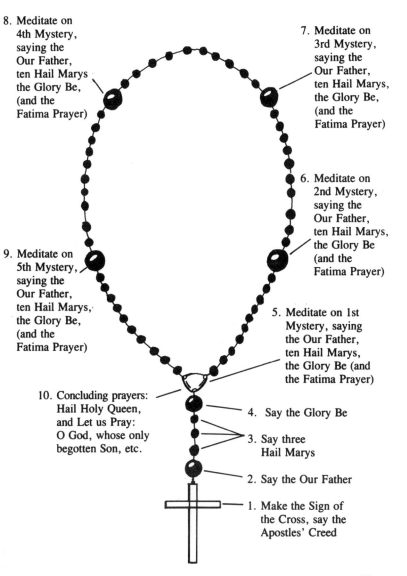

8. Meditate on 4th Mystery, saying the Our Father, ten Hail Marys the Glory Be, (and the Fatima Prayer)

7. Meditate on 3rd Mystery, saying the Our Father, ten Hail Marys, the Glory Be, (and the Fatima Prayer)

6. Meditate on 2nd Mystery, saying the Our Father, ten Hail Marys, the Glory Be (and the Fatima Prayer)

9. Meditate on 5th Mystery, saying the Our Father, ten Hail Marys, the Glory Be, (and the Fatima Prayer)

5. Meditate on 1st Mystery, saying the Our Father, ten Hail Marys, the Glory Be (and the Fatima Prayer)

10. Concluding prayers: Hail Holy Queen, and Let us Pray: O God, whose only begotten Son, etc.

4. Say the Glory Be

3. Say three Hail Marys

2. Say the Our Father

1. Make the Sign of the Cross, say the Apostles' Creed

5. *The 'Mysteries'*.

Each is to be prayed while saying a 'decade' (the block of prayer comprising Our Father, ten Hail Marys, Glory be). Those who say five Mysteries a day usually do it in this way:

the *Joyful* on Monday and Thursday;
the *Sorrowful* on Tuesday and Friday;
the *Glorious* on Wednesday, and Saturday, and on Sunday (except in Advent when the *Joyful* would be said, and in Lent when it would be the *Sorrowful*).

A brief explanation of each Mystery now follows, together with a few lines of relevant scripture. As has been suggested, such a brief passage could well be read before each decade, at least while one is learning the way to pray the rosary.

The Five Joyful Mysteries

1. *The Annunciation*: The Angel Gabriel announces to the Virgin Mary that God wishes her to become the Mother of his Son. Mary obeys with humility.

    "And when the angels had come to her, he said, 'Hail, full of grace, the Lord is with thee. Blessed art thou among women' " (*Luke 1, 28*)

2. *The Visitation*: Mary visits St Elizabeth, who is to be the mother of St John the Baptist. She assists Elizabeth for three months.

    "And Elizabeth was filled with the Holy Spirit, and cried out with a loud voice, saying, 'Blessed art thou among women and blessed is the fruit of thy womb!' " (*Luke 1, 41–42*)

3. *The Birth of Christ*: Jesus Christ, the Son of God, is born in a stable. His Mother places him in a manger. Shepherds and Wise Men visit him.

    "And she brought forth her firstborn son, and wrapped him in swaddling clothes, and laid him in a manger, because there was no room for them in the inn." (*Luke 2, 7*)

4. *The Presentation*: Mary and Joseph take the Child Jesus to the Temple at Jerusalem to present him to his Heavenly Father.

"And when the days of her purification were fulfilled according to the Law of Moses, they took him up to Jerusalem to present him to the Lord." (*Luke 2, 22—23*)

5 . *The Finding of the Child Jesus in the Temple*: Having lost Jesus, Mary and Joseph seek him. After three days they find him in the Temple.

"And it came to pass after three days, that they found him in the temple, sitting in the midst of the teachers, both listening to them and asking them questions." (*Luke 2, 46*)

The Five Sorrowful Mysteries

1 . *The Agony in the Garden*: Jesus prays in the Garden of Olives. The thought of his coming sufferings and of our sins causes him to sweat blood.

"And his sweat became as drops of blood running down upon the ground. And rising from prayer he came to the disciples, and found them sleeping for sorrow." (*Luke 22, 44—45*)

2 . *The Scourging at the Pillar*: Jesus is stripped, bound to a pillar, and scourged until his body is covered with wounds and blood.

"Pilate then took Jesus and had him scourged." (*John 19, 1*)

3 . *The Crowning with Thorns*: A crown of thorns is pressed onto the head of Jesus. His eyes fill with tears and blood. He is mocked and spat upon.

"And they stripped him and put on him a scarlet cloak; and plaiting a crown of thorns, they put it on his head, and a reed into his right hand." (*Matthew 27, 28—29*)

4 . *The Carrying of the Cross*: Jesus carries his heavy cross to Calvary. Mary makes the stations of the cross with her suffering Son.

"And bearing the cross for himself, he went forth to the place called the Skull, in Hebrew, Golgotha." (*John 19, 17*)

5 . *The Crucifixion*: Nailed to the cross, Jesus after three hours of agony, dies in the presence of his Mother.

" And Jesus cried out with a loud voice and said, 'Father, into thy hands I commend my spirit.' And having said this he expired." (*Luke 23, 46*)

The Five Glorious Mysteries

1. *The Resurrection*: Victorious over death, Jesus rises from the grave glorious and immortal, on Easter Sunday. He reopens the gates of Heaven.

   "He has risen, he is not here. Behold the place where they laid him." (*Mark 16, 6*)

2. *The Ascension*: Forty days after his Resurrection, Jesus ascends, in the presence of his Mother and his disciples, into Heaven.

   "So then the Lord, after he had spoken to them, was taken up into heaven, and sits at the right hand of God." (*Mark 16, 19*)

3. *The Descent of the Holy Spirit*: Ten days after the Ascension, the Holy Spirit descends in tongues of fire upon Mary and the disciples.

   "And they were all filled with the Holy Spirit and began to speak in foreign tongues, even as the Holy Spirit prompted them to speak." (*Acts 2, 4*)

4. *The Assumption of Mary into Heaven*: The apostles go to the tomb of Mary but find that the angels had borne their Queen to Heaven.

   "And a great sign appeared in heaven: a woman clothed with the sun, and the moon was under her feet, and upon her head a crown of twelve stars."(*Apocalypse 12, 1*)

5. *The Crowning of Mary as Queen of Heaven*: The Mother of God, to the joy of all the angels and saints, is crowned Queen of Heaven by her Son.

   "Thou art the glory of Jerusalem . . . the honour of our people . . . the hand of the Lord hath strengthened thee, and therefore thou shalt be blessed forever . . ." (*Judith 15, 10–11*)

A Synopsis of 'Styles' of Prayer and Some Appropriate 'Methods'

1. *Informal Prayer*

This wide term can include the whole spirituality known to St Ignatius as 'Finding God in all things', and to his colleague Nadal as 'Contemplation in action'. The following practices are appropriate:

   (i) Renewal of consecration and of good intention (cf. The *'Morning Offering'*, and aspects of devotion to the Sacred Heart specified in the *Apostleship of Prayer*).

  (ii) Ejaculatory prayer.

 (iii) Prayer at 'stimulus points' of Beauty, Ugliness, Joy, Pain.

 (iv) The practice of the Presence of God (cf. *The Practice of the Presence of God*, Brother Lawrence, O.C.D.).

  (v) The practice of 'the Sacrament of the Present Moment' (cf. *Abandonment to Divine Providence*, De Caussade, S.J.).

 (vi) Conscious obedience (cf. *The Mysticism of Obedience*, Leeming, S.J.).

2. *The Mass*

3. *The Word of God*

   (i) Scripture reading.

  (ii) Bible services.

 (iii) Derivative prayer (spiritual reading in the strict sense;

meditation on the mysteries of Christ's life; Rosary; Stations of the Cross).

4. *Group Prayer*

   (i) Pentecostal and 'charismatic' (cf. *Did you receive the Spirit?*, Tugwell, O. P.).

   (ii) Shared prayer.

   (iii) Community discernment (cf. Futtrell, S. J.).

   (iv) Sharing the Word.

   (v) Chapter of Faults.

   (vi) Revision of Life.

5. *Devotion to the Blessed Sacrament:*

   (i) Benediction, Exposition, 'Forty Hours',

   (ii) Corpus Christi Procession,

   (iii) Visits to the Blessed Sacrament.

6. *The Sacraments:*

   (i) Baptism,

   (ii) Confession,

   (iii) Eucharist,

   (iv) Confirmation,

   (v) Matrimony,

   (vi) Holy Orders,

   (vii) Anointing of the Sick.

(It is not fiction to claim a method of prayer for each Sacrament. These, and a 'shadow sacrament', and a 'life-prayer', related to each could be postulated. Here it is well to note that in each Sacrament the 'prayer' should advert to five elements: a material thing, bringing a touch of Christ, through the Church, consecrating a part of God's creation as a 'vehicle' of grace, with an element of permanence.)

7. The 'Prayer of the Church', or Divine Office, or Breviary

8. Sacramentals

In a wide sense, the term can include prayer arising from the right use of almost any material object, even unblessed, as a means of grace. The following are examples:

(i) Ikons,

(ii) Relics,

(iii) Holy Water,

(iv) Blessed objects,

(v) Crucifixes, statues, pictures, medals, scapulars,

(vi) Lourdes water,

(vii) Food (which after Grace becomes spiritual nourishment as well).

9. Liturgy

(i) Liturgy in the stricter sense:
Mass,
Sacraments,
Office, Prayer of the Church,
Benediction.

(ii) Para-liturgy includes:
Processions,
Bible Vigils,
Penance Service.

10. Formal Private Prayer

This has been treated at greater length in chapters 2, 3, and 4, under the headings of 'Theory', 'Preliminaries', and 'Structures in Prayer, and Methods', so the list which follows has already been amplified in the text:

(i) Structures:
Aids to attention.
A.C.T.S.; A.L.T.A.R.

(ii) Methods – vocal:
Talking to God,
Listed intercession.

(iii) Methods – primarily for Bible prayer:
Meditation,
Pondering words of vocal prayer,
Rosary,
Stations of the Cross,
Applications of the Senses,
Ignatian Contemplation,
Prayer of Images,
The 'Fool's Prayer',
Scripture 'Bombing'.

(iv) Methods – primarily for 'arid contemplation':
Breathing Method,
The Jesus Prayer,
Deep Recollection,
Prayer by Mediators,
Recollection by Mood (or 'Centering Prayer').

Appendix 2:

Three Practical Formats for Group Prayer

1. *General scheme* (time: say thirty minutes for twelve people)

(1) *Act of Faith in Christ's Presence*
(Chairman speaks for three minutes or so, long enough for all to make the act of faith, on the lines of chapter 6, no. 5).

(2) *A few lines of Scripture*
(Not too much, or people will turn it into Scripture study, or want to prepare the text and then lecture on it. No comment on it. Someone else reads it for a second time, so that it may be truly listened to.)

(3) *Silent Prayer*
Chairman: 'Now we pray silently for five or ten minutes. We could pray starting at Christ's presence among us, or at the text, or at Christ's presence in each of us, or in any way we choose.'

(4) *Shared Prayer* (time: say ten minutes)
Chairman: 'Now we can speak out loud if we want to. We do not try to think of things to say, but if we think Christ would like us to speak out loud from our prayer, we do. We ask ourselves, "If I could see and hear Christ among us what would I want to say?" ' (cf. chapter 6 no. 5).

(5) *Conclusion*
Chairman: 'We end with a Glory Be. It is to thank Christ for his presence; to ask his blessing on those who have brought him to us; to lift up to the Father, with Christ, all that has been said, and all that has been in our hearts; to remind us that he is still with us even though our prayer is over; to ask him to send us his Spirit, with all his Gifts.'

Silent Prayer of 'Repetition' can usefully be inserted in the time of Shared Prayer. Repetition in Ignatian language is to go back to the point of Consolation or Desolation. The object is to open oneself to what might have been a movement from the Spirit. In Group Prayer, the Consolations often arise from what other people say, and Repetition helps one to listen, ponder – and meet others.

2. *Detailed scheme for beginners* (time: say fifty minutes for twelve people).

This can be suitable for absolute beginners. It is 'safe', but at the same time invites one to move a long way towards openness in Christ's presence.

(1) *Act of Faith in Christ's Presence*

(2) A few lines of Scripture.

(3) *Silent Prayer* (five minutes).

(4) *Reflection* (two minutes).
   Chairman: 'We now reflect on the past few minutes of prayer. We look to see what, if anything, we have had from God. To do that, we ask ourselves two questions: "How did it go? How was it between me and God?"
   The first question is easy – "I was bored; I was sleepy; I found it easy etc. etc." The second is impossible – but still worth trying to answer – "I felt close to God: I tried to realise Christ was here; I was sorry for my sins; I didn't feel a thing etc." '

(5) *Shared Reflection* (fifteen minutes).
   Chairman: 'Now we go round the ring, each person answering these two questions if they want to. No obligation to answer – anyone can "pass". If you do answer, try to keep it down to 90 seconds.'

(6) *'Repetition'* – see above (five minutes).

(7) *Shared Prayer* (ten minutes).

(8) Conclusion.

3. *Scheme for prayer-discussion*

(1) *Act of Faith in Christ's Presence.*

(2) *Proposal of subject.*
e.g. Chairman: 'Let us take two questions: What do I think God wants from *me* about help for the Third World? What do I think God wants from *us*?'

(3) *Silent Prayer.*

(4) Shared Reflection (again, very short answers, say ninety seconds).

(5) *Repetition.* (Prefaced if necessary by Chairman reading out the headings of what has been said.)

(6) *Shared Prayer.*
Chairman: 'Now we speak if we wish; if possible we want to get God's light on how to make it practical.'

(7) Chairman sums up.

(8) Conclusion.

A Note. Much structure is not necessarily useful even at the beginning. Please read chapter 6 no. 6.

The Act of Faith in Christ's presence 'in the midst' is all important. Please re-read chapter 6 no. 5.

Appendix 3:

A Form of Penance Service

1. *Purpose and Nature*

The Penance Service described here is designed to bring out certain elements in the Sacrament — notably the ecclesial dimension — which are normally not obvious; to make it easy for participants to make a serious act of contrition; to help them to understand a little better the implications of *metanoia*; to make people 'feel they've been properly'; above all, it serves to bring back to the Sacrament many who have been long away.

The Service should not last more than an hour at most; therefore with a previous explanation lasting twenty minutes, one priest could in that time hear, say, fifteen penitents; two priests thirty, and so on.

An obvious disadvantage is that the Confessions would be rapid and there would not be time for spiritual direction. On the other hand, especially without the screen, the penitents could easily be invited back for a talk outside Confession; also, it is hoped that what is lost for some in this way is more than made up for the majority by the effective use of Sacramentals and a fuller Liturgy. Anyway, in practice, how many penitents ever get direction in the Box?

The effect of the Service does depend on Liturgy and Sacramentals. If whoever explains it (and this need not be the actual Confessor) does not understand and believe in the principles of liturgical worship and the Sacramentals used, and can only succeed in turning it into a rubrical formalism, he should not try to handle it.

The Liturgy and the Sacramentals used get their impact by being done or used before other people as witnesses. The actions are a public pledging of oneself. This is why the implications must be spelled out for the people to understand.

2. Arrangements

On the sanctuary, under the Tabernacle if possible and facing it, or before the Blessed Sacrament exposed, a prie-dieu. Beside it, facing Tabernacle, chair for the Priest. If appropriate *(but preferably not)* a light screen between Priest and penitent. If more than one Priest is hearing, chairs as appropriate; but ensure that nothing could be overheard. (A note on Nuns: even the old Canon Law permits screenless Confessions when a Priest, for sufficient reason, designates a place for Confession.)

On the Altar, or beside the Tabernacle, two lighted candles. At the entrance to the Sanctuary, a bowl of holy water.

Halfway up the aisle, a table, and lying on it a fairly large crucifix.

In the back benches of the church (or far enough away to be out of earshot) the group of prospective penitents. Back of them, a Reader with Bible, Rosary, Hymnbook.

3. Explanation

Probably twenty minutes is long enough for explanations, but the Service does give a good chance to give instruction on Confession (cf. chapter 8). Here is only an outline of the explanation of the Liturgy.

'There are five things you can do during this Penance Service. You must not feel obliged to do any of them — except the first, which is simply to listen to God's Word.'

'So first, while you are sitting there, you will have read to you passages from the Bible. The readings will be interspersed with decades of the Rosary; please join in these. The Bible readings give you God's idea of sin and forgiveness — and include Passion readings.'

(*Note:* I do believe that the 'background' should be genuinely prayerful. Especially with young people, avoid 'entertaining' them or appealing to anything less than a genuine liturgical experience.)

'The second thing is this: one by one you could come up *here* — pick up this crucifix, and kiss it — *thus.* You will probably feel foolish doing this — excellent! It is a public act of contrition: it is to say "before all of you here, I publicly show that I am a sinner, and I kiss this crucifix to tell you all *and God* that I am grateful to

Christ for what he has done for me, and that I am deeply sorry for my sins.".'

(*Note:* before one can explain the point of kissing Christ's image to others, one must obviously be entirely convinced oneself. This Penance Service, in its use of Sacramentals, does require this.)

'After you have kissed the Cross you could go back to your place. Or, if you want to, you could go on up, right up *here*, before the Blessed Sacrament and kneel down *here*. What is that a sign of? It is to show all present, *and God*, that, in a context of repentance, you want to go to where Christ's Body is as a sign that you are sorry. And here, you can ask for Christ's Blessing from the Priest. And that is a sign to all, and to yourself, that you know the Church (whose minister the Priest is) is where Christ is to be found.'

(*Note:* when someone comes up for a blessing, it is of course a most opportune moment for a very short word of congratulation and help by the Priest.)

'Then, on your way back, fourthly you can do this. Take Holy Water from this bowl *here*, and sign yourself with it. What does this mean?'

(Here go on to teach about the Sign of the Cross; how the use of Holy Water is a prayer of gratitude for Baptism, of petition to be *fecundated* by the Holy Spirit, of petition to be washed clean by Christ's Blood (cf. chapter 7).)

'Or, fifthly, instead of asking for the Priest's blessing, you could have gone to Confession instead.'

Explain that it would probably not take longer than asking for a blessing, since the Priest would give the 'Short Form'; explain that the Penance would be to go back and join the others for the rest of the Service; explain that no one from the back would know whether you had gone for a blessing or for Confession; explain that Confessions will be heard in the Box at such and such a time for those who don't wish to go now; explain everything that prospective penitents – who may reasonably be uneasy – will need reassurance about. Explain that anyone who has been away a long time will probably never have an easier chance than now. Explain (cf. chapter 8) how the Sacrament works and how to tell the sins (in so doing you make an examination of conscience for the people). Explain above all the *effects* of the Sacrament.

4. *Background prayer and readings*

This forms the first of the five possible events of the Penance Service, and the cumulative effect of hearing God's Word in silence and undisturbed is immense. Taped music or taped readings are not so effective.

On occasion litany-type prayers helping examination of conscience could be interspersed. But it seems to me vital that the people should mostly not have to hold anything or read anything: their eyes must be free to watch. Singing is *not* always useful here; the hymn is read by the reader, not sung by the people.

All handbooks to the 'New Rite' of Penance give selection of readings for the 'Second Rite'. Here are others. A good weight of reading devoted to help contrition is obviously sensible: the tendency to leap *at once* to the Resurrection is regrettable.

Lk. 7: 36–50.
First Sorrowful Mystery – The Agony in the Garden.

Lk. 15: 3–10.
Second Sorrowful Mystery – The Scourging at the Pillar.

'O Sacred Head Ill-used' (vv. 1–3) (recited by the reader).
Third Sorrowful Mystery – The Crowning with Thorns.

Mt. 27: 28–33.
Fourth Sorrowful Mystery – The Carrying of the Cross.

Jn. 19: 25–30.
Fifth Sorrowful Mystery – The Crucifixion and Death of Our Lord.

'O Sacred Head Ill-used (vv. 4–5) (recited).

Is. 53.

Ps. 50 (Miserere).

Ps. 21 (My God, My God).

Rom. 6: 5–11.
First Glorious Mystery – The Resurrection.

Col. 3: 1–10.

Acts 1: 8–11.
Second Glorious Mystery – The Ascension.

Rom. 8: 9–17.
Third Glorious Mystery – The Descent of the Holy Spirit.

1 Thess. 4: 15–18.
Fourth Glorious Mystery – The Assumption.

Lk. 1: 45–55.
Fifth Glorious Mystery – The Crowning of Our Lady in Heaven and the Glory of all the Saints.

5. Conclusion

The readings stop when no one is left to go. Then the Priest comes down and walks up the aisle to the people, each of whom returned to his place after going to Confession. Then he says: 'I will now say over you all the words the Priest can say while giving Absolution, but I will change the words from being a prayer that God *should* do something to a statement that he *has* done something. In the short form I used, you will have missed the implications. What I am saying now is not therefore an absolution, but – if you have been to Confession – a reasonable statement of your present position before God.'

'. . . through the ministry of the Church God *has* given you pardon and peace, and the Priest absolved you from your sins in the name of the Father and of the Son and of the Holy Spirit'.

'The Passion of Our Lord Jesus Christ, the merits of the Blessed Virgin Mary and of all the Saints, whatever good you do, whatever evil you will suffer, *will* gain for you the remission of your sins, an increase of grace, and *will* gain for you the reward of eternal life.'

'And now to end the Service I give you a last blessing with this crucifix we have all kissed.'

Note: To listen passively to God's word is a beautiful way of prayer. To watch others kiss the crucifix and be absolved is immensely strengthening. Too much activity, in the way of singing; too much having to hold books or bits of paper, is regrettable for the people. And gimmicks, or canned Simon and Garfunkel, are verging on the deplorable.

Examination of Conscience; Vocabulary

1. Examination of Conscience, and some Vocabulary

The major headings may be useful for most people. The fourth, 'The Roots of Sin', is probably the most useful; there are things that underlie the sins we tell the Priest in Confession.

The minor headings may be useful for those who have to teach others. Sometimes vocabulary itself is a difficulty.

(i) Things directly against God:
Concealing a serious sin in Confession.
Sacrilegious Communion.
Denial of any point of the Faith.
Mockery of God or of the things of God.
Dabbling in the occult (seances, ouija boards, etc.).
Mass of obligation (e.g. Sunday) missed?
Lack of confidence in God.
Lack of gratitude to God.
Not living in his presence.
Taking his name in vain.
Slackness in prayer.

(ii) Things involving others:
Things said or done which hurt.
Stealing, dishonesty.
Speaking unkindly of others.
Telling lies which have hurt.
Giving bad example.

(iii) Things to do with 'Life':
Drinking too much.
Driving when having drunk too much.
Smoking too much.

Over-eating.

Drugs taken wrongly.

Abortion.

In time of war, use of weapons immorally.

Sexual sin
- slackness in dealing with thoughts or feelings against purity;
- use of contraceptives in the marriage act; withdrawal;
- sinned against purity by using pornographic material;
- ... with another; by immodest touches and kisses;
- ... with another; it was the complete act.

(iv) The Roots of Sin:

Moral Cowardice.

Self
- self indulgence (wrong pleasure);
- self aggrandisement (wrong ambition, envy, seeking the limelight, seeking to dominate, seeking discomfiture at the expense of others).

Culpable blindness.

Not *really* knowing God *really* loves me
- not trusting God.

A Method of Going to Confession

This scheme is probably not the best possible. But the great rule with the 'New Rite' is that the penitent should be free to go in any way which pleases *him*. There is liberty. This way is a common method. Old people need not fear they will do it wrongly.

1. *Before Confession:*
    Ask God for help. Examine Conscience. Act of Contrition.
    ('O my God, because you are so good, I am very sorry that I have sinned against you; and with your help I will not sin again'.)

2. *With the Priest:*
    'Please Father forgive me for I have sinned. It is ... since my last Confession. These are my sins ....'
    End 'I tell God I am sorry for these and all the sins of my life. That's all, Father.'
    The Priest gives you the penance.
    Then say the Act of Contrition (see above).

3. *After Confession:*
    Say the penance. Act of Contrition. Great gratitude to God. Ask help for the future.